LADIES
WHO
LAUNCH

LADIES WHO LAUNCH

*An Innovative Program That Will Help You
Get Your Dreams Off the Ground*

Victoria Colligan and Beth Schoenfeldt
with Amy Swift

 St. Martin's Griffin ⚹ New York

www.stmartins.com

Library of Congress Cataloging-in-Publication Data

Colligan, Victoria.
    Ladies who launch : an innovative program that will help you get your dreams off the ground / by Victoria Colligan and Beth Schoenfeldt with Amy Swift.
        p. cm.
    ISBN-13: 978-0-312-35955-3
    ISBN-10: 0-312-35955-1
    1. New business enterprises. 2. Entrepreneurship. 3. Businesswomen. 4. Success in business. I. Schoenfeldt, Beth. II. Swift, Amy. III. Title.

HD62.5.C637 2007
658.1'1082—dc22

                                                                2007003012

First St. Martin's Griffin Edition: May 2008

10 9 8 7 6 5 4 3 2 1

*This book is dedicated to
the magnificent women in our Ladies Who Launch network
and to all the women who have launched before us;
you inspire us every day.*

Contents

Part III: The Ladies Who Launch Community and Resources

Acknowledgments

Each of us has been blessed with a loving family and an abundance of friends, loved ones, treasured guides, advisors, and teachers who have supported us from the very beginning when our idea was just a seed. It would not have been possible for us to take the risks and fulfill our vision without each and every one of you. You know who you are, and for you, the biggest hug and kiss, and our deep and appreciative thanks.

Thank you to the thousands of women in our Ladies Who Launch network and our Ladies Who Launch Incubators, and especially to our Ladies Who Launch Incubator leaders in cities around the world. We wouldn't be anywhere without your inspiration and we live in awe of all that you have accomplished.

Thank you to Beata, Karen, and Nicole, our launch support team, who work with us on a daily basis and have believed in us from the start. Your dedication gives Ladies Who Launch the platform to fly; you have all of our gratitude.

Thank you to our agent, Alison Fargis of Stonesong Press, and to all of the people at St. Martin's Press for your energy, commitment, and support in making this book all that we imagined it could be!

Last but not least, we may be called *Ladies* Who Launch, but we love men wholeheartedly, especially the men in our lives: Owen, Scott, and Josh. Thank you for your unending enthusiasm and support.

Love,
Beth, Victoria, and Amy

Authors' Note

Caution! By following the guidelines in this book, you will change your life as you know it. Do not read any further if you are not interested in turning your dreams into reality. This book is designed solely for those who are ready to move forward in their lives and let the world know who they are and what they are truly capable of achieving.

Introduction

If you want to pop the lid off anything you ever thought you couldn't do, shouldn't have, or couldn't achieve, you've bought the right book. All the tools you need to ignite a fire under a long-smoldering dream, or to catapult a lifestyle, relationship, or career to a higher level, are right here. Women tend to think of dreams as bigger than themselves, pies in the sky, morsels of imagination saved for a rainy day—in other words, out of reach. Well, guess what? *Ladies Who Launch* will reprogram how you think about your dreams so that they are as real as the coffee you drink each morning. They're real and they're all yours! To be truly happy and inspired by the life you're living, you can take steps to wake up and launch your dreams right now. It is time to start believing that you can have what you really want. With the help of *Ladies Who Launch*, you will.

Why Not You?

Were you ever told to stop dreaming that you could be the next Kate Spade, the next Nora Ephron, the next yoga master, the next Nicole Kidman, the next Fortune 500 CEO, the next Oprah, the next It girl, or the next business profiled on *Daily Candy? Ladies Who Launch* says, "Why not you?" Someone is going to break out and be recognized for achieving success and enjoying the fruits of her dreaming; it might as well be someone as fabulous and deserving as you. In fact, it couldn't happen to a better person! If you have dreams (and we know you do), then there is an entrepreneurial spirit inside you waiting to break free. The entrepreneurial spirit can include the traditional definition of entrepreneurship and revolve around launching a business, or that spirit can encompass the enthusiasm and ambition all entrepreneurs possess and be channeled into any part of your life.

Our culture tends to discourage women from reaching for the stars and embracing our creativity. The messages we are more likely to receive are: "Work hard," "Stay out of trouble," "Get good grades," "Play it safe," and "Be responsible." Because of these admonitions, it becomes easy to let years of precious life go by without writing that book, pitching that idea, creating that loving relationship, or simply decorating the house exactly the way you want it. Your "inner entrepreneur," the creative engine that can transform your dreams into reality, is kept in check.

Ladies Who Launch is about unlocking your dreams and letting them out into the world, allowing them to be as big as they were meant to be. Rather than suppressing your desires because you don't want to be too bold, too proud, too much, too greedy, we say let them loose and allow them to grow! If you have reached a level of success, we dare you to go to the next level; you never want to stop looking forward to the next interesting thing. While you should appreciate every delicious bit of what you have, it is absolutely necessary to keep striving for more. Without desires and dreams, the flame in your furnace dies out and life becomes mediocre, inspiration fades, depression sets in, and you stop creating and achieving. However, wanting more goes far beyond material possessions and brings you deep into the realm of well-being and happiness, a place where you can design your life exactly as you'd like it to be, and tap into your creative and entrepreneurial spirit. First, you have to realize that you can have a say in your life; you can escape the expectations that you learned from your school, work, family, and friends. You have to appreciate that you can

custom-design your unique path and that no matter what you were
told, you are a brilliant, innovative being.

The Program

Ladies Who Launch is a movement. Yes, it's an in-person and online
network for women to connect, grow, and celebrate. But it's also a way
of thinking and being that discards the idea that there is only one
way to launch, one way to live, or one way to be creative. Ladies Who
Launch is an agreement between a woman and herself that says, "No
matter what, I want my life to keep moving forward, keep getting better, and keep being closer to my dreams."

We've designed a four-step program called the Incubator to propel
the intrinsic yearning every woman has to launch her life, to embrace
her creativity, to move forward into territory only she has the desire
to claim for herself. The Ladies Who Launch program is a conduit for
creativity. Women place their dreams inside this virtual greenhouse
and discover a supportive environment for their precious thoughts,
ideas, and visions. The imaginings can take any form—great relationships, a fulfilling career, a creative outlet, an enriching family
experience, financial freedom, or being the queen of your kingdom (however you define that)—and through the Ladies Who
Launch Incubator program, the dreams grow until they are hatched
into reality.

Any desire can be put into this Incubator model and expanded.
Some of the real women whose lives are bigger and better than they
ever imagined by utilizing the Ladies Who Launch Incubator include:

- Karen Mudrick, who moves to a new city and wants to expand
  her social life, spice up her nightlife, and befriend a more diverse crowd. She bravely jumps into the Ladies Who Launch
  Incubator and within days finds herself out at chic parties,
  spending weekends in a beach house, and creating a Rolodex
  of close friends.

- Robin Wilson, a former executive recruiter who decides she wants to build a business as an owner's representative for home renovation—an unusual role in the world of construction and architecture. With only a couple of clients under her belt, she joins the Ladies Who Launch Incubator, and within three months has more than twenty clients for her company, Robin Wilson Home, as well as feature articles on her business in magazines and newspapers across the country. Ultimately, this led to a whole new launch project of giant proportions: Robin was selected by Hearst Magazines to be its spokesperson for its home-oriented publications. This lady can't be stopped!

- A corporate executive, Carolynn Kutz has a dream of breaking out of her cubicle and getting behind the camera to shoot a movie. With only an inkling of an idea about what, where, and how, she pitches her story to the women in the Ladies Who Launch Incubator, who receive it with wild appreciation and excitement. Amazingly, several others in the group also want to get into the film game. Carolynn is soon on the sidewalks of New York, collaborating with the women in Ladies Who Launch to act, write, and produce the movie for a film competition she courageously dares to enter. Lights, camera, action, she comes in second place!

- Emily Farber is tired of working for a PR agency, uninspired by her daily routine and lethargic lunches over a keyboard. She envisions pitching the press from a grand marble desk in her home, spending time with her new puppy, and continuing her work in communications but on her own time and terms. In a few short months she has her own PR business, Hudson Communications, with a growing client list that appreciates her boutique (independent) agency. They respect and appreciate her at-home work environment and ability to be flexible and execute outside the normal confines of the agency-client contract.

- Jennifer Bessier has a love affair with cooking and decides to grow her culinary hobby into a Web site for the kitchen-challenged. Her Web site, www.chefsline.com, has a mission to empower people in the kitchen. Its flagship offering is a national culinary hotline that offers personalized menu planning, cooking, and wine consultations for busy people seeking to have more fun (and success) in the kitchen and make cooking a more integral part of their lives.

- Ann Greenberg starts her own sweater company, Rouge, in the face of a saturated retail market. Despite warnings from others, she launches with tremendous success, and within a year is selling in Bloomingdale's By Mail and Neiman Marcus Direct. She has been featured in *Women's Wear Daily* and is now free to pursue other press outlets. Indicators said no but the Incubator said yes.

Are any of these dreams like your own? You could easily be one of these stories but not if you let your ideas remain dormant because of an overcommitted schedule, fear of failure, or a world-weary approach to life.

The Ladies Who Launch Dream

Our business and this book were developed out of our actual experience. We were (and still are) following our dreams, discovering our true passions, taking huge leaps, and most important, drawing on the energy of our friends, family, acquaintances, and anyone who was willing to give us any input in creating our company, Ladies Who Launch. Our point in sharing our own story is to help you begin to understand how a project, relationship, job, or situation can manifest itself in an inherently feminine way. We have discovered out of our own experience and that of women who have participated in our Incubators that women approach change, creativity, and business quite differently from men. This is not a bad thing! In fact, it worked for us—it can work for you, too.

We didn't begin this journey with a specific result or even a very clear vision in mind, and we certainly didn't have a business plan.

What we both had was a very strong and almost overwhelming desire to create something that would make us excited to get out of bed each morning and add a little light and love into the world. Sure, we wanted to make money. We love making money! But we also wanted to make an impact on the world and spend our time doing something that was fulfilling in every way. What really drove us to break out of the corporate mold and launch was creating a lifestyle that gave us freedom and flexibility. We are both hard workers with strong work ethics, but we wanted to be successful on our terms, creating time for the things that are important to us, including our family, our friends, traveling, philanthropy, yoga, and the world around us. What we realized, after working for corporations and for start-ups, was that unless the business was a true reflection of our own dreams, no one else's business would make us as happy as one that was our sole creation. We knew our path would be entrepreneurial and our mission would be to build on an idea that would allow us to stand on our own beautiful feet.

Coincidentally, we not only started our individual journeys toward making our dreams come true at the same time, but we both had similar ideas. Victoria set out to launch a magazine called *Avanti,* which means "movement" in Italian. Meanwhile, Beth created FLOinc, an organization whose mission was to move people forward and get them into the "flow" of their lives. We were both solo-preneurs (before we married our businesses together) and wanted to support and forge connections for other women going through the same process. After looking high and low, neither of us was able to find exactly what we were looking for in terms of an organization or resource that combined creativity, business, fun, and lifestyle. We discovered that we weren't alone. We asked around and found that many women wanted to break out of the corporate mold, use their creativity, do something fulfilling every day, enjoy their femininity, have fun, and connect with other like-minded, motivated, and creative women. There seemed to be nowhere to turn. Networking as a concept and even as a word was never something either of us had found at all enticing or supportive. It involved images of conference rooms, hotel lobbies, business cards, and name tags, and felt boring, tedious, strained, and unnatural to us.

So we did what many women do; we saw a need and sought to address it.

Subsequently, our businesses were born. Victoria turned her magazine concept into www.ladieswholaunch.com, an online resource for women that features entrepreneurial success stories with a focus on lifestyle and creativity. Beth added a workshop called the Incubator to her menu of courses as a way to spend time with like-minded and motivated women and to help them crank up the volume on desires and dreams. Both concepts grew organically and quickly; the Ladies Who Launch subscriber base grew as women across the world signed up to receive their weekly dose of inspiration in the form of a Featured Lady who had herself successfully launched. The Incubator, starting in New York City, became a word-of-mouth phenomenon as women flocked to the program. From marriage proposals to business partnerships and photography treks in Southeast Asia, life got rosier for the women in the Incubator, which evolved into that networking organization that we had dreamed of, combining entrepreneurship, creativity, and lifestyle. Together, we are able to provide the network and resources that women need to launch, both online and offline.

This process wasn't easy. We learned, in hard but ultimately positive ways, as we went along. We both self-financed our dreams without any guarantee of success. And although we both went to business school, we found the approach we used for launching our dreams to be in almost direct conflict with what we had been taught. When we took the leap of independence, it was an exhilarating but terrifying experience. When you are in the middle of creating something brand-new, it can be almost paralyzing. We'll be the first to admit that we've had everything from cold sweats to insomnia thinking about how to advance our brilliant ideas. Even when you know something works and it has proven itself to you in various outstanding ways, there is always a pinch of doubt. Will they use it? Will they like it? We truly believed that women would grow and thrive and become believers by coming to Ladies Who Launch and going through the Incubator process, but at the same time we wondered, will it work? Are there women out there who crave the resources and community we do, without the corporate networking model in place?

Luckily, not only did people come, they spread the word, told their friends, and most important, saw results. Every time a woman associated with Ladies Who Launch takes a tiny step toward her goal, gets a feature article published, makes her first 100K sale, makes a new friend, or gets engaged, it launches the rest of us higher and paves the way for others to follow. Five years later we have a thriving and growing business that changes lives every single day. We have had thousands of women all over the world take part in the Ladies Who Launch Incubator program and we are thrilled with the remarkable women that Ladies Who Launch attracts. Each, like you, is dynamic, creative, supportive, entrepreneurial, ambitious, and most important, kind and generous. They are ready to take major steps in their lives and understand that doing it together is a lot more fun than doing it alone.

What we realized through this experience is that when you're enthusiastic about an idea and going for it with all your heart and passion, the universe, people, and circumstances line up behind you to make it possible. Family and friends contributed to our efforts, but also people we barely knew but who felt our enthusiasm have given us great ideas, connected us with their friends and associates, and spread the word that ultimately became the foundation for Ladies Who Launch. Had we tried to do this on our own it would have been so much more difficult; we might have spent many years getting up the courage to actually go for it. Our cowriter Amy Swift's journey has run parallel to ours. Not only has she launched a business as a brilliant and talented writer and brand-identity guru, but she is also the Ladies Who launch Incubator leader in Los Angeles. From the very beginning Amy has championed us, helped us write, created course names and descriptions, and developed our brand. In fact, early on, over lunch at the Cafeteria restaurant in New York City, Beth was explaining the workshop she dreamed of creating for all of her friends who had inspired her and who had helped her start her business. She imagined creating a forum so that they, too, could give birth to their dreams. Amy said, "Like an Incubator?" and so it began. Amy is not only a writer, she is a collaborator who has brought her unique vision and insight into our world, and whose vision so complements ours that we solicit her two cents whenever possible. We know that with her help, whatever we are doing will be that much better and bigger because together we create something even more wonderful than we could have on our own.

Great Ladies Launch Alike

After going through the process of starting our businesses, working with thousands of women across the country, and connecting with thousands more women through our Web site, we realized that our experiences starting Ladies Who Launch were in many ways typical, and in keeping with the feminine style, of other women who start businesses and other projects. We were so happy to learn that we weren't crazy or unusual for approaching our business in our organic way. In fact, when we talked to or studied so many women that we admire, from maternity designer Liz Lange, to Carley Roney from The Knot, to Discovery Toys founder Lane Nemeth, we found that they, too, followed an unconventional process in launching, and we began to document these trends. After doing our research and synthesizing all the data, we realized that we were onto something that no one ever told us and that they didn't teach in business school.

We discovered that:

- Women want to feel fulfilled, have fun, enjoy their femininity, and not sacrifice these desires for financial success. Women are redefining the very notion of success as they incorporate many elements, not just a career or family, and want to be able to celebrate their personal creativity in whatever manifestation that means.
- Women are natural connectors, they derive fulfillment from relationships, and use them to move forward and execute ideas. They rely on relationships to get information, advice, and social interaction.
- Women tend to treat creative projects and new businesses like their children: they become emotionally attached. They fall in love with their ideas and with making them happen, and

are unlikely to give away equity in their own businesses or projects easily. They will sacrifice extreme growth to retain sole ownership because they define themselves through their projects and derive extreme personal fulfillment from them. They view relationships emotionally; responding to what *feels* right as opposed to what *looks* right on paper.

· Maybe there isn't a glass ceiling after all. Women typically do not wish to invest time and energy in relationships or projects they don't have a passion for, nor will they climb the corporate ladder only for the promise of more money or prestige. Oftentimes they might not want to do what it takes to get to the top of an organization because being there doesn't reflect their ultimate goal of balance and happiness.

· Women multitask and tend to be time-starved, juggling families, businesses, and self-fulfillment. Women value giving time and attention to all the various components in their lives, viewing "success" through their ability to include everything in their lifestyle. Routines and structure provide a framework for constant change and evolution.

· Women tend to be nonlinear thinkers, meaning they don't always know where they are headed when they start a project, nor do they feel compelled to need to know. They move from passion and intuition and see where it takes them.

We came to realize that while the process of starting our companies happened organically, the process is actually definable, understandable, and comparable to the path of many launching women. We then realized that we could translate this process into a workshop, developing resources for others to follow to make that path easier and clearer. This process has become our Ladies Who Launch Incubator program.

Not only have we seen hundreds of our Ladies Who Launch Incubator participants go through a similar process, we sent a questionnaire to our entire subscriber base and surveyed hundreds of men and women outside of it to understand what commonalities are shared by successful people who have turned ideas, dreams, and desires into reality.

Transforming a Dream: The Common Denominators

1. They can clearly *imagine it.* They imagined achieving what they desired and had a clear vision of where they wanted to be, even without knowing how to get there.
2. They created the unique voice or point of view that helped them *speak it* and stand out in the crowd, usually building on their inherent talent.
3. They *act on it,* taking the actions and steps toward making it happen, and persevering through setbacks.
4. The ones we admire the most, *celebrate it.* They enjoy every step of the process, including the days they feel close to falling off the edge.

Key Lessons from Successful Women

- **Success is not a solo activity**. For anyone who has taken a dream to the next level or expanded it to greatness, there have been numerous people that they can point to—teachers, mentors, colleagues, friends—who have counseled them, supported them, and boosted their confidence.
- Truly successful people are not suffering, they are **having fun and they are in the flow**. They say yes to life. It isn't that they aren't working hard, interested in making a lot of money, or don't have tension headaches once in a while, but they are doing something that they love, so the hard work actually becomes pleasurable. The right people and situations are drawn to them. Their enthusiasm is contagious.
- Successful people understand that success requires **process**. They are continually evolving; they have big dreams, clear intentions, and are willing to go down any and every path to achieve their highest goals. The process is as fun as the result.
- The most successful **trust their intuition**. They don't listen to societal conventions, adhere to limitations, or let obstacles get in their way. They imagine themselves reaching the highest pinnacle and they don't waver or shrink from their lofty goal.

- They are willing to **take the leap** and close all other doors that will keep them from their dream. They put all their eggs in one basket because they know that they will not be happy otherwise.

If you're not an entrepreneur by definition, or don't want to be, we've discovered that by using the examples of women who have launched before us and applying the techniques used for starting a business through the Ladies Who Launch method you can build *anything.* This means any area of your beautiful life that needs attention, nourishment, or magic.

And if you feel stuck in your life or your project, or your dream or "next move" is not immediately clear, we understand your frustration and this book will be especially valuable to you. As you read, we are going to ask you to do something counterintuitive, to let yourself stay in the uncomfortable place. Just like the old saying, "What you resist persists," the harder you try to get out of a difficult spot the longer you will stay stuck. The best thing you can do is to diligently complete all the exercises in this book, follow the Incubator process, and put yourself around other motivated and entrepreneurial women for inspiration. Most important, don't give up. Have fun, and take it easy on yourself. Nothing stays exactly the same for very long . . . which should be comforting.

The point of *Ladies Who Launch* is to help you to manifest your undertaking. We'll help you realize that you aren't alone in the way that you approach launching, and understand exactly how to create an environment where you can develop and nurture your dreams and desires. It's time to banish the could'ves, would'ves, and should'ves. It's time to get you ready to *launch!*

Part I
....

Great Ladies Launch Alike

The Feminine Approach to Launching

1
....

Introduction to Launching

We don't like to limit any area of our lives that could be launched. For one person it's a business, for another it's a social life, and for someone else it might be an exercise program. Launching means getting anything off the ground, or at least into a more evolved state than it's currently in. Anything can be launched once you understand the specifics of how to do it. You will no longer be the person who catches herself, years down the road, wishing she'd learned French, made a documentary, or started a matchmaking business. Once you have the tools to launch you will have the tools to get anything up and running, now and for the rest of your life.

Our philosophy is that launching doesn't have to mean writing a business plan, selling the house, moving to another city, or even leaving your job. Launching is a state of mind, a way of thinking. If you don't have the luxury to go away to a deserted island to write your novel, there is no reason you can't get started in some significant way today. Too often we put off starting something because it seems too far-fetched or would take too much energy. Some of us don't know how to follow through or fear it might change our lives too much. The reality is that when you have a map of how to get somewhere, it immediately seems much more attainable. If Everest were simply some Goliath peak in the sky, with no guidelines on how to scale it, do you think anyone other than crazy explorers would dare climb to the top?

> **Authors' Note:** How long can you stand to let your dreams go unnoticed? What daydream comes to you again and again? If wishing could make it so, what would be yours? Is there something you're waiting for? How long are you willing to wait? How long is too long? Is now soon enough?

We're giving you a map. You can go to the base camp or all the way to the summit. How high to go will always be up to you, but our experience has shown that once a woman figures out the launching process, she can't be stopped. Launching becomes a verb that describes both her appetite for creativity and her ability to execute.

We are fanatical about launching because we know that the movement toward your desires and dreams is the key to happiness and self-esteem. Mihaly Csikszentmihalyi, in his landmark book *Flow: The Psychology of Optimal Experience,* says it best when he writes:

> Contrary to what we usually believe, the best moments in our lives are not the passive, receptive, relaxing times—although such experiences can also be enjoyable, if we have worked hard to attain them. The best moments usually occur when a person's body or mind is stretched to its limits in a voluntary effort to accomplish something difficult and worthwhile.

He goes on to say that optimal experience is something that we make happen and that is how you get into the flow of your life. Nothing is more active than launching; it is how you make things happen. It's critical for your self-esteem and happiness to get you thinking about your dream right from the start, and get it out there as soon as possible. It's one thing to have a dream locked somewhere in your head, be a decent human being, and feel good about yourself and your life. It's quite another to let it out so that it can *actually happen* and so you can see what this does to how you feel about youself.

To further support our theories that women launch in different ways and for different reasons than men, and that launching brings happiness and fulfillment, we conducted a nationwide survey of Ladies within our subscriber base (women who have or who are developing an entrepreneurial spirit). We then surveyed corporate women outside our subscriber base as well as gentlemen, both those in corporate environments and others launching outside the corporate arena. The results were fascinating, challenging, and at times surprising. We also surveyed women who have been profiled on www.ladieswholaunch.com (the Featured Ladies) as our "success" stories. We consider them successful for reasons beyond their bank accounts or business models. These women are living their dreams; they enjoy amazingly rich lifestyles, have fascinating, industrious friends and supportive families, many have children, and naturally many of them have been rewarded with the financial success they so certainly deserve for their efforts. Key, though, to each of them, is the sense that a dream was imagined and carried out. Their particular "project" could have just as easily ended up a passing fancy . . . not a nationally known brand!

Launching and Self-Esteem

We knew that we felt better about ourselves after launching our businesses, so we wondered if launching could be a prescription for boosting self-esteem and happiness. In our survey we asked all the women and men if they felt good about themselves, and we all know that people who felt good about themselves are happier and have higher self-esteem.

The answer was a resounding yes, launching is good for self-esteem, *especially* for women. Look at the difference between the self-esteem index of Launching Ladies compared to their friends in the corporate world. Wouldn't you like to feel almost 20 percent better? This isn't to say that you feel down or bad, you just might feel better if you are taking actions that lead to a new venture. When you're birthing something, from a new room in the house to a lemonade stand, your inner magic wand is in action. It's not about *what,* but more about *doing.* This means that going out in the world, making things happen,

LADIES WHO LAUNCH SURVEY

Do You Feel Good About Yourself?

	Featured Ladies*:	Launching Ladies:	Corporate Ladies with a Side Launch:	Corporate Ladies:	Launching Gentlemen:	Corporate Gentlemen:
Strongly Agree	61.3%	51.2%	43.2%	32.0%	43.1%	27.6%
Agree	38.7%	42.8%	49.3%	56.0%	51.0%	65.6%
Neutral	0%	5.6%	3.0%	12.0%	2.0%	3.4%
Disagree	0%	.4%	4.5%	0%	3.9%	3.4%
Strongly Disagree	0%	0%	0%	0%	0%	0%

*Ladies featured as "success stories" on www.ladieswholaunch.com.

and stirring the pot is more than just fun and possibly lucrative; it could save you big bucks on therapy bills and also fill in a few of the holes that crop up and make you feel like something might be missing.

Shades of Gray

Some people see launching as black or white. You may be thinking, "I can't launch because if I do, everything else will fall apart, or things will change so much that I won't be able to handle them. Conversely, if I don't, life will stay the same forever and fail to inspire me sometime down the road." Propelling ideas outward doesn't require sacrifice and perpetual change. The bottom line here is that reaching for dreams makes you feel good, and for a long time. So, if launching is so good for your self-esteem, why wouldn't you launch? We asked that question of our corporate sisters and brothers in the context of entrepreneurship, one part of the launching concept, to find out what it is that holds people back.

It is scary to leave the stability of a paycheck and your health insur-

LADIES WHO LAUNCH SURVEY*

What Is Preventing You from Starting a Business or Going Freelance? (Select Two.)

	Corporate Ladies:	Corporate Gentlemen:
It is just too scary to leave the stability of a regular paycheck.	43.1%	33.3%
I would like to but I don't know what I would do.	31.4%	42.4%
I don't want to lose my health benefits and other benefits.	27.5%	9.1%
It would be way too much work to start and maintain a business.	17.6%	3%
I am just not interested in the responsibility.	15.7%	3%
I don't have any idea how to start and run a business.	13.7%	27.3%

*Only the top results are listed.

ance and to put yourself on the line, to take that risk, when you may have a family at home or not a lot of cash in the bank. If you are in the corporate boat and not ready to get off, this book will help you think about launching in a slightly different way, and you can even use these skills and mind-set within a corporation. In the traditional model it's been black and white—either you're an entrepreneur or working in a corporation. We see things in a beautiful shade of Weimaraner gray. This gray area could be working full time in the corporate world, and possibly doing something toward your passion on the side, or perhaps pursuing something creative as a hobby. Looking back to the self-esteem question, those who work in a corporate environment and who are pursuing a dream and launching something on the side feel better about themselves. When we talk about launching, it's easy to think we are only addressing it in the "start your own gig" sphere. This is partly true, but not completely. We know that women can launch in hundreds of ways that don't necessarily involve work at all. There is a mind-set of launching that involves figuring out what you love and infusing some action in your life that isn't necessarily pragmatic, obligatory, or purely functional. You may also be someone who has a burning desire to launch but doesn't know exactly what it is you would like to do. If that's the case, this book will help you sort it out.

. . .

Portrait of a Lady

When Caren Henry Glatcz, founder of ecokiss, joined the Ladies Who Launch Incubator, she had an idea to launch a store that sold all environmentally friendly green products. Her background and experience was in advertising and marketing for a large conglomerate, but she was feeling increasingly uninspired and unfulfilled. Caren took the leap when she realized she could apply skills she already had toward helping small businesses with brand-related strategies, while slowly moving forward with ecokiss. Not only did the consulting bring in extra income, but in this capacity she was able to trade her marketing skills for products and services that she needed to launch ecokiss. She traded brand development work for a cabinet she needed in her space; she wrote a press release for someone in the Incubator in exchange for participation at an event that would help promote her company. Her creative bargaining finally paid off. ecokiss, based in Cleveland, Ohio, opened its doors as a store within the well-known health-conscious store Mustard Seed Market in April 2006 with plans to grow online and in other creative venues.

Moving Beyond Tradition

Sometimes we ladies don't feel "right" about the way we approach our lives or our businesses. Our premise is that this is because we live in a male-standard society. What we mean is that in most cases, the feminine voice has been left out of the laws, rules, religions, and corporations that govern and create infrastructure in our communities. We call this male standard the "traditional model" throughout the book. We're happy to report that the feminine voice has become more prominent over the last twenty years, but as women discover and acknowledge that their way of working, living, and being differs from men, they are becoming even more impassioned and interested in finding a new approach that mirrors their natural inclinations. There is a new way to look at your lifestyle, your relationships, your money, and the overall way you design your life. We call it the Ladies Who Launch way. We hope to fully document this feminine approach so that you learn to trust yourself more and feel right about launching your dreams and desires.

Some of you might feel stuck from having lived in the traditional model for so long and may need a major traditional model detox. Someone suffering from being tradition bound has gone numb, become a cog in the wheel, and possibly let her style and femininity get kicked to the curb. She doesn't question her routine, her nine-to-five hours, her life and time dictated to her by others. She's so asleep that she can't see what another way of living and working might look like. Sometimes she lets herself go and might put on extra weight, go out less, isolate herself, feel endlessly tired, and be despondent about the future. She also probably wrestles with a nagging feeling of not being good enough, of anxiety over getting fired or staying in an unfulfilling relationship, of "Where would I go if I didn't have this?" Those less affected might be able to express curiosity about "What might be out there, if not this?" No matter what your level of traditional toxicity, there is a path to recovery. The first step is to question your current situation. You might not be in the corporate environment; in fact, you could be at home raising kids, thinking about "What's next?" You can be in any stage of your life, from your twenties to transitioning toward retirement, and find yourself wondering "What if?" or "I don't know what I want, but I want something!"

Often, upon realizing that we have been living (and for some, suffering) in the traditional model, we can feel deceived, angry, disturbed, or confused about why certain environments (such as corporate structures) feel so constraining. The traditional model is dominant in our society, creating a huge imbalance between the masculine and the feminine in our everyday lives. Upon deeper reflection you will see that many of us have been living in a world of self-doubt and low self-esteem, feeling guilty about who we are and what we think about, as well as having a complete lack of confidence in many of the decisions we make. Though many of us make the decisions anyway, seemingly acting true to ourselves, these decisions are often clouded with extreme doubt and anxiety, energy-sapping emotions that can impede creative forward movement. We start a business or launch a creative project but become riddled with self-doubt in the process. Should I be doing this? Will I make any money? Do I have what it takes to be successful? For many of us, it is a process to regain our confidence, to see another way, to consider a different perspective. We usually don't acknowledge or understand that it's usually circumstances and cultural messaging that has made us feel this way. We think it's just our own constitution, our own doubt. So we live, and adjust. Women are typically good at managing change and appeasing conflict, even if it's inside their own minds!

Before you can move toward launching and creating anything and everything you desire in your life, and before we introduce you to the Ladies Who Launch Incubator model that will help you get there, it's important to have an understanding of how great ladies launch alike so that you can use what naturally comes easily to you to propel yourself forward.

After interviewing droves of successful women for *Ladies Who Launch*, surveying our entire subscriber list, and working with thousands of women in the Ladies Who Launch Incubator, we saw distinctly that not only do women launch differently than men, they launch for different reasons as well. We wondered why we hadn't read about this or learned about these differences in college, business school, or any type of school for that matter. When we were launching Ladies Who Launch, we set out to connect with hundreds of women. We were relieved to find that we were not alone, that our successful sisters were thinking and going through the same process that we were, but nobody was talking about it; nobody was pulling all the information together. What we have found is that these differences between how men and women launch amount to much more than a trend; we would define it as a movement, a new way of being, and *Ladies Who Launch* is the first book to define this approach. When we talk about these differences to the women in our Ladies Who Launch Incubator, they are relieved and feel validated. What's more, after much digging and doing our own research, we find that there are hard statistics to support the existence and validity of this feminine approach.

We discovered the following about the ways that women are launching:

- Women are launching for lifestyle reasons; more than anything they want control over their creativity and schedule (they want to do what they want to do when they want to do it).
- Women are natural connectors and Ladies use this natural resource to launch.
- It is *not* solely about the money. The primary motivation for women launching is not money, it's passion.
- Launchers are in touch with their inherent creativity and intuition and place trust in these resources (which often can't be seen, only felt) to wade through obstacles and take leaps of faith.

In reading this book, we hope that you feel validated in the way that you think about and approach your life, feel less alone in the world, and become more connected to your sisters who are leading the way.

Launchwork

Note on launchwork: these exercises are meant to inspire you to discover more about yourself. The key is to have as much fun as possible with them. Try to approach each learning experience with a sense of adventure and playfulness. It's part of the process that will lead to great rewards. We enthusiastically suggest you buy a launch journal to keep all your exercises together in one place; you can track your progress, growth, movement, and self-discovery.

Traditional Model Detox

In order to launch as high and as far as we know you are capable, you need a clean slate and a clear mind. Releasing some of the patterns of thoughts and actions that have kept you stuck in the traditional model will help. If you remember the movie *The Matrix,* the humans who lived in the Matrix were literally stuck in their patterns and had to be deprogrammed in order to re-enter "reality." Detox can be difficult and sometimes painful, but it is worth it to deprogram and break free of ideas, behaviors, and patterns that will no longer serve you. You can then make room in your life and your space to move forward free and clear. Here are some ways to do this:

Clear your space. Look around you and see what can be thrown away, given away, or recycled. Look beyond material items and consider the people in your life who may be holding you back. Sometimes a closet needs weeding out, a kitchen pantry needs some love, or a toxic and negative person needs to be left behind. Many people who start new businesses clean out filing cabinets and desks as a first step because they don't want to think about making a sale or hatching a single idea until they have a clear space for what's to come. Dig into the corners and detox your house, office, bedroom (under the bed is typically a place where things get dumped, and unless it's organized, many a feng shui expert contends it creates unwanted heavy energy), and tackle any areas you can handle. Think about the people around you: are they supporting you in reaching your goals or sucking the energy out of your life? It can be hard to let go. The first step toward cleaning up is acknowledging what *needs* to go. This process may carry on throughout the time it takes you to read this book or through the next year. Take as long as you want; just be sure to clear out the cobwebs and make room for what's next.

Clear your calendar. Many of us are in debt with our time, overly committed and booked for weeks on end. This exercise helps you to look at your schedule and see what can be eliminated, so that you have time to not only read this book and do the exercises, but also to launch your heart's desire. Are you having too many coffee meetings with people you don't particularly want to spend time with? Is there a way someone else can help you with a car pool? Could time be saved by getting up thirty minutes earlier (and going to bed earlier, too)? Think carefully about what is unnecessary and what you really aren't that interested in continuing. Do you have too many activities or commitments that no longer serve you? Do you need to resign from some boards, extricate yourself from a book club, or scale back the number of evenings you slave over dinner? When you start to take a closer look at how you are spending your time or what you are engaging in, some of these activities may appear worthy on the surface: You are on the board of the art museum, in charge of your child's homeroom activities, or partaking in a monthly book club. It might just be the wrong time in your life for any one of these worthy (but overbearing) engagements. Or they may be energy drains, meaning they have no place in your creative life and they have become more of a burden or a dreaded activity than something that provides you with meaning or fulfillment. Most people find they have quite a few appointments they have little or no interest in keeping. If friends who are continually negative or untrustworthy get the boot during this phase, be prepared for their negative reactions to you and to what you are doing. They may be sad or disappointed that they no longer feel connected to you. Acknowledge their disappointment to yourself (and to them if it comes up), but keep moving. You know instinctively where you are going. Because this is a gradual process that will require your time and energy, be aware of how you are spending these precious resources. Cleaning out can be hard, even emotional! But it's worth it.

Clear your mind. The last area to wring out is your thought process, which will require cleaning up some of your existing beliefs about the meaning of launching. We're not asking you to become a blank slate and forget everything you've ever learned, we're just asking you to be conscious of what ways of thinking might have held you back in the past, and to consider letting go of those thoughts. Here is what one thirty-something Incubatress put on her list of thought detox:

No one in my family is an entrepreneur, which means I don't
    have what it takes.
Launching something means it has to be a business.
I don't have the money.
I don't know how to write a business plan.
I'm not creative.
Launching means changing everything.
I have nothing to launch.

Write down anything that comes to mind that might keep you from
launching. From financial concerns to time constraints, anything can
go on your list. Once you get it all down in your launch journal, look
it over, and write the opposite!

For example:

No one in my family is an entrepreneur, which means I don't have what it takes.	Being the first entrepreneur in my family will be fun and even more exciting.
Launching something means it has to be a business.	I can launch everything in my life from my social life to my knitting hobby, and possibly one day a business.
I don't have the money.	Without money I will have to be more creative and resourceful, which is a great quality for launching.
I don't know how to write a business plan.	I can launch without a business plan and learn when I need to.
I'm not creative.	I am creative in my own way and I am going to learn how to tap into that creativity.
Launching means changing everything.	I can launch something in my free time or on the weekends, or even launch within the expectations of my job.
I have nothing to launch.	I will discover my passion and launch.

The detoxing process can feel scary and hard as you go through it,
but when you finish you will feel clear, free, and ready to launch.

Maintain your focus on this process and remind yourself daily that you are in detox, and see how life makes room for what you really need, and how it easily lets go of what's extraneous.

LAUNCHING BOOK RECOMMENDATIONS FOR DETOX

The Raw Food Detox Diet by Natalia Rose. This book inspired us to examine every area of our lives for toxins and excess. A great physical inspiration, the book offers relevant parallels with respect to making space, getting rid of old stuff, and putting the newer, more evolved choices into the physical and mental machine.

Flow: The Psychology of Optimal Experience by Mihaly Csikszentmihalyi. A fascinating read on many levels, but primarily a good guide to identifying happiness and fulfillment in your everyday life.

LAUNCHING MOVIE RECOMMENDATIONS FOR DETOX

The Matrix. Redefine and examine the reality you're living in by noticing the many levels of reality that exist in this movie. It's possible that your reality could be altered for the better by opening your mind to alternate ways of thinking. They are always there, but are you noticing them?

The Corporation, directed by Mark Achbar and Jennifer Abbott, and written by Joel Bakan. This documentary explores traditional corporations and exposes some of the major flaws inside them. Beware, this is a disturbing, provocative, and astute assessment of the corporate personality.

2

· · · · · · · · ·

Launching as a Lifestyle Choice

What woman doesn't want a life filled with wagonloads of love, a host of interesting friends, luxurious and adventurous vacations, and a wickedly abundant financial portfolio? Add the freedom and flexibility to do what she wants when she wants and you have something that resembles perfection. A characteristic of successful Ladies Who Launch that we see across the board is an overwhelming desire to live a fulfilled, soulful, passion-filled life. You may have that same impulse: the need to fall in love with your life so that you wouldn't trade it for anything . . . including all the money in the world. When we say love your life we mean not just your boyfriend, husband, dog, or job, but every single part of your life, from the sheets you sleep on to the tea you drink, to the way you spend your weekends and the way you make a living. Most people want a life that's fulfilling, a life that invites waking up to each day, a life that engages your brain, emotions, sense of play, romance, or even makes you want to be a kid again. One component of this picture is freedom; freedom to own your schedule, decide when you want to eat, work, go to a museum, paint, have coffee with a friend, and so on. This doesn't mean you have to tell your kids to make their own sandwiches or e-mail the boss that you're quitting, but it does mean looking at the status quo and deciding if it could be different. Do you want the liberty and flexibility to do what you want when you want to do it? We would be shocked if you didn't say yes, because most people crave the ability to own their own schedule, but just haven't yet figured out how to achieve that level of freedom. While we want more control over our time, there are many women, and men for that matter, who don't have that ability. From our research and experience, we see that many women are fitting themselves into the lives that society dictates. They are not actively deciding when and how they live their lives. Not only do they work nine to five, and are culturally or socially encouraged to comply with a dress code that doesn't fit their personal style, often their leisure-time activities and child-rearing are deeply influenced by a cultural standard that may not match their true belief system. Their mismatch with the "norm" may not be conscious—most people haven't even given themselves the luxury of thinking, dreaming, or picturing what kind of life they would like to lead because nobody ever gave them the option to do so. Some have pictured it, but their picture got buried under too many have-to-do expectations.

This chapter is dedicated to showing you the differences between how women fare inside traditional structures such as corporations, versus independent-alternative structures, and how that impacts their well-being and lifestyle. Most people (97 percent of the women we surveyed) have worked for someone else, likely a midsize to large corporation, at some point in their careers. If you don't work in a corporate environment now, have given it all up, are a stay-at-home mom, or are currently launching your own business, this information is valuable because it will legitimize much of what you've suspected all along. We'll also explain why the desire to have a complete life has women launching businesses at twice the rate of men, according to the Center for Women's Business Research, and how you may be able to get in on the action.

Before we get started, the first step is to access and acknowledge your way of thinking (I can have something different in my life and not lose anything), and then to realize that yes, you can take charge of your life (I am the one behind the wheel even though I feel like a slave to my schedule or background).

The following survey questions, and those that appear at the beginning of each chapter in Part I of this book, are designed to better help you evaluate where you currently stand, *not* to make you feel bad about yourself. Think about it: it's impossible to chart a course in a new direction or make any changes in your life until you know where you are! You'll also be able to compare some of your answers with what we heard from our survey respondents—both women and men.

LADIES WHO LAUNCH SURVEY

Are You Caught in the Traditional Model?

The traditional model emphasizes productivity and efficiency over all else, including fulfillment, enjoyment, and personal style.

If money were not a concern I would still be doing what I am doing.	___Yes	___No
I feel fulfilled and passionate about what I am doing.	___Yes	___No
I wake up every morning looking forward to my day.	___Yes	___No
I feel as though work reflects my true passion.	___Yes	___No
My work fits into my ideal lifestyle.	___Yes	___No
I feel like I am living the life I was born to lead.	___Yes	___No
I have the flexibility in my life to plan my day the way that I like.	___Yes	___No
I am able to take time off whenever I like.	___Yes	___No
I take very good care of myself.	___Yes	___No
I spend all the time that I desire with my friends and family.	___Yes	___No
I feel a sense of "getting somewhere" or fulfilling a bigger picture.	___Yes	___No
I would say that I am "having it all."	___Yes	___No

If you answered yes to all of these questions, congratulations, you are the rare creature who has the highest level of fulfillment and you are likely to go even higher. If you answered no to even one of these questions, there is some room for change in your life. Think of it as just needing to do a little redecorating or a renovation of your life. Like any construction job, however, there may be a little mess before the masterpiece. Don't be afraid of this mess, either! Sometimes a few things get deconstructed before new ideas and actions can take hold.

The Corporate Path?

Maybe you've arrived at a point in your life when you start to question your path. Perhaps you are like so many of the women we surveyed who have happily worked in a corporate environment or similarly uninspiring circumstances, but who have been thinking about what their long-term life plans look like, and wondering, "Will I be doing this forever?" Maybe you're a mother who can't decide whether to go back to work, launch your own project, or stay home with the kids. Maybe you're happy in your job but feel there is some other creative outlet that you would like to explore. It's possible that you could also be at a life transition point and be contemplating your next incarnation. It is natural for a woman to look down the road and wonder, "Is there more? What should I expect from myself? What do I want?"

Sometimes these reflections can be addressed by launching inside the current structure. Launching doesn't mean throwing absolutely everything away and starting anew. In fact, the best way to launch is to use the pad you're sitting on right now. Launching inside a corporation can mean presenting a new initiative to the boss and then running with it, taking on another role, or even assuming a more junior position in an entirely different area in order to advance in the direction of your interest. There are people who give up successful careers as interior decorators, teachers, salespeople, or accountants to sort mail in the mailroom. Why? Because launching for them means doing whatever it takes to get moving in the right direction, even if it means starting at the very bottom of the food chain. Most of us witnessed our own mothers become successful in their chosen careers, or have had other close examples of successful businesswomen to follow. Thanks to women's rights, virtually every door is open to us; there are women at the top of the legal profession, heading Fortune 500 companies, heading huge nonprofits, running anything from movie studios to construction companies. Women have now surpassed men in enrollment in advanced schooling in law and medicine! The fastest growth for women-owned businesses is occurring in nontraditional fields for women, including construction (30 percent growth), transportation, communications, public utilities (20 percent growth), and agricultural services (24 percent growth), according to the Center for Women's Business Research. So clearly, there is definitely launching taking place inside both corporations and within nontraditional fields for women. However, if we don't want to take a path inside the folds of a traditional company, we may question our drive for success or think something is wrong with us. If you're talented and brilliant (as we know that you are), why wouldn't you want to pursue a top position in a company? Society would tell us that the ultimate goal is to get to the top of whatever you choose to do, to get promoted to CFO, manage the entire sales force, or become chairman of the board. If you have different ambitions outside of the traditional model, what does that say about you? We would argue that a desire for the nontraditional route is a pretty good problem to have! It means that our lives have evolved to a point where we can sit at the crossroads and take one of many paths, including getting to the top if we so desire.

More choices mean more responsibility, but making a choice can happen when you're twenty-five, thirty-five, or sixty. Choosing one path over another is truly not a question of age but an answer to the question of how do you want your life to look, feel, taste, and be? We posed the first survey question you answered at the beginning of the chapter to both women and men.

The results on the next page indicate that it is clearly not about money. In fact, we could conclude that if money were not a concern, let's say someone won the lottery (a man or a woman), they would flee corporate America as fast as they could. But women would be putting on their track shoes and running the fastest. The myth is that if money were no object you would take off, leave work behind, and live differently. Notice that fewer launchers would leave their businesses if money were no object. They want to keep doing what they are already doing. That's a pretty favorable testament to launching!

The Corporate Reality

LADIES WHO LAUNCH SURVEY

If Money Were Not a Concern, Would You Be Doing What You Are Doing Now?

	Launching Ladies:	Corporate Ladies:	Launching Gentlemen:	Corporate Gentlemen:
Yes	82.9%	11.1%	76.9%	14.3%
No	5.9%	74.1%	10.8%	64.3%
Not Sure	11.2%	14.8%	12.3%	21.4%

Many of us graduated from college or business schools with visions of long corporate careers dancing in our heads. Then encounters with various levels of bureaucracy sour the vision. Bosses can be competitive, managers uncooperative, and other employees divisive, all of which makes it tough to accomplish tasks, carry out initiatives, or thrive inside an environment that does not inherently foster or celebrate creativity. From what we have been told, even when women truly enjoy their corporate environment they often have a nagging feeling that there is something missing. They fantasize about the day when they might break out on their own.

We have discovered that the corporate reality for many (both women and men) is bleak and restrictive. Getting to the top levels of a corporation is a daunting prospect with long hours, unstable environments, possible layoffs, and a time-card-punching mentality that is not at all conducive to juggling family, social life, or creative hobbies. Additionally, what we hear from many women in corporate jobs is that they do not feel they have a voice. But given the overriding culture of most corporations, it's hard for any one person to have a voice except for a few key people. It's also easy for them to feel they've lost their vision, lost sight of goals, because corporations don't necessarily foster a sense of individual achievement unless they're under wise management or careful nurturing. Overall, this doesn't leave them feeling all that fulfilled. In some cases, they don't necessarily want to leave, but they wish there were more opportunities to express creativity or at least glean acknowledgment for what they do well. Feeling invisible or unremarkable is easy in a big company, especially with little room to prove otherwise. Those who stay against their deeper desire to do something else often feel as if they don't have any other options, or don't feel that the options they do consider (such as entrepreneurship or freelancing) are realistic.

We, too, have tried that corporate routine and felt uninspired, creatively flat, and continually frustrated by bureaucracy. We wondered if there was something wrong with us, and questioned why we didn't feel driven to move up this chain of command; we even considered the possibility that we had authority issues. This isn't totally surprising when you consider "authority" to be someone in the company whose orders you have to obey but whose vision may not make sense to you. Is that so wrong?

But . . . on the Bright Side of Corporations

LADIES WHO LAUNCH SURVEY*

To Entrepreneurs:

	Launching Ladies:	Launching Gentlemen:
Have you ever worked for a corporation or someone else? If yes, how do you feel about your corporate experience? (Select all that apply.)	97.1%	100%
I truly enjoyed my experience.	17.1%	26.3%
It was a great training ground.	60%	78.9%
I felt that there was a glass ceiling at work.	20.2%	18.4%
I felt creatively stifled.	41.9%	42.1%
I hated everything about it.	12.8%	13.2%

*Only the top responses are listed.

The positive things we hear (besides the health benefits) are that corporations are a great training ground for current aspirations and future endeavors. Whatever you decide to do, any gig inside an existing organization, big or small, gives you a landscape to learn from. Charging straight out of school, pregnancy, travels, and so on, into entrepreneurship can be fine for some people, but others want to see other companies in motion before they take the plunge. Corporate experience is like boot camp, and it almost always informs the future, but it is not always negative or constraining. There are companies out there with corporate structures that ditch the old models, making employees never want to leave. But not many.

Again, despite men seeming to be just slightly more enamored with their corporate experiences than women, the results are rather consistent. In the corporate environment, women and men learn how to make initiatives happen; they get real-world experience in finance, sales, marketing, PR, and management inside a living, breathing, operational company. Some love the structure of office hours and a "plan" devised by a higher chain of command. It gives them a ready-made framework from which to live their lives, and in a way more freedom because of that structure and the lack of stress that can come from being on your own. Most women, whether they know it consciously or not, require creativity to feel fulfilled, but not everyone fits the literal definition of an entrepreneur. We have seen examples of women using their entrepreneurial energy to launch within the corporate structure, provided they feel genuine satisfaction and acknowledgment from their efforts. Many women find happiness launching a business or a creative project on the side of their primary job. A 2006 *Los Angeles Times* article profiled different groups of fitness instructors who love their day jobs (accountant, lawyer, shop owner) but who also enjoy the outlet of teaching, exercise, and motivating people several times a week. In many ways, the corporate model works as it relates to a career path for a certain period of their lives because coming out of school, and for some time after that, it offers structure, steady pay, and a direction to go. You have to do something to earn money, and corporate jobs are a big, and often exciting, opportunity. A corporate job may time out, however, after a woman has children and needs more flexibility, or even after she's got some career life under her belt and starts to think about what she truly wants for the next twenty years. What people want at twenty-two and what they want at thirty-two and forty-two can be wildly different. The litmus test for when a corporate job has run its course has everything to do with excitement, a sense of possibility, of curiosity, and motivation. When these factors wane and going to work becomes merely an obstacle to living the rest of your life, other options need to be explored. We contend that as long as it's useful, a corporate gig is cool.

. . .

Portrait of a Lady
A CORPORATE ENTREPRENEUR

Jane Carpenter Lamb, vice president of marketing with American Greetings Interactive, has found a way to launch within the corporate structure. Using extensive market research and a need she identified as not being met for herself and her friends, Jane and her team came up with the idea of launching Bloom by AG, an online card division that is a little more hip, stylish, and fun than the typical American Greetings products. The best part about launching within the corporate structure? The many resources, financial and otherwise, available. The worst part? The ultimate lack of control over the timing and objectives of launching new products. Although Jane has to remind herself that ultimately some decisions are simply not up to her, she has found creative fulfillment in being able to access the resources of a large company to push innovative and original ideas forward in ways that she might not otherwise have been able to do on a limited budget. American Greetings has provided her with an entrepreneurial framework and an openness in which to do so. She also has been able to structure a flexible work schedule that allows her precious time with her two small children.

The Glass Ceiling?

"I couldn't sustain it."
—Colleen Wolfe of the Minneapolis Ladies Who Launch Incubator,
a mother with three children who left a top position at Qwest Communications that
required at least two weeks of travel per month

**"I didn't experience a glass ceiling but too often
found a sticky floor."**
—Sherry Harris, former executive vice president for the Morgan Hotel Group
who left to pursue her "soul work"

According to a Babson College study of the top one hundred Massachusetts businesses owned or led by women, female CEOs are most likely to start or run their own businesses out of a desire for personal achievement (85 percent) and to challenge themselves (80 percent). Conventional wisdom has held that women start businesses to overcome the glass ceiling in corporate America, or out of economic necessity. On the contrary, economic necessity ranks last on women's list of motivations for starting or leading their businesses. Only a third cite avoiding the glass ceiling as a motivation. As much as women love to spend money, have money, feel secure, and be surrounded by nice things, money was not the primary motivator for breaking free from the clutches of corporations. If all they wanted was financial security, they would stay put! They may not rise to CEO, but they would certainly still pay the mortgage, and in some pretty nice neighborhoods, too.

Many women have been told there is a glass ceiling and that this is the reason that very few women have ever made it to the top of corporate America. The idea was that men were somehow holding us down and keeping us from moving up the ladder or through the ceiling. Many women were thought to have given up because they couldn't break through to management positions or above. It is true, not many women are at the top of Fortune 500 companies, but we question the conclusion that women are not at the top because of the glass ceiling theory.

LADIES WHO LAUNCH SURVEY

To Corporate Women: Do You Want to Get to the Top of Your Organization?

	Corporate Ladies:	Corporate Gentlemen:
Yes, I would love to do what it takes to become CEO.	5.7%	26.2%
No, getting to the top of my organization would be too much work.	11.3%	9.5%
I am more interested in making money than getting to the top.	35.8%	11.9%
I am more interested in feeling fulfilled by my job than whether or not I get to the top.	47.2%	52.4%

If fewer than 6 percent of women desire to do what it takes to get to the top, whether they believe in the glass ceiling or not, then a glass ceiling is more folklore than reality. Ultimately, what is motivating the women in corporations is not "doing what it takes to become a CEO." Overwhelmingly, their goal is to feel inspired by their career or, if they are going to be working all day, to at least make a big salary. Men are much more likely to be interested in doing what it takes to get to the top, but many are not all that interested, either. Getting to the top is not most people's greatest aspiration. Intrinsic job satisfactions are much more important.

We began to wonder if there was a glass ceiling after all. Most people we know didn't want to be at the top of the corporate ladder—in fact, many wanted to leave corporate life. Maybe we want to believe in the glass ceiling because it gives us an excuse to bow out or not even try. We in no way want to denigrate those men and women who have chosen a path that takes them to the corner office—it's just a lot of hard work. We genuinely respect those who have achieved great status inside companies such as IBM, Hewlett-Packard, and Disney. It's possible that very few people have that kind of perseverance, drive, and single-minded focus, especially when there are no guarantees that will theoretically get you to the top. We so admire and tip our hats to the women who have made it to this pinnacle and appear to be enjoying the ride; for example, Meg Whitman, president and CEO of eBay, Andrea Jung, president and CEO of Avon, and Shelly Lazarus, chairman and CEO of Ogilvy & Mather.

We also admire so many of the women who have deliberately chosen to step away from corporate life, seeking out alternative structures and more flexible lifestyles. It's not about right or wrong, it's about what fits and what doesn't. Just like a boyfriend, a dress, a house, or a food group. You might have loved Mountain Dew for breakfast at twenty-one, but at thirty-one, it occurs to you that overloading on sugar and caffeine isn't in your best interests at seven in the morning.

Choosing a Launching Life

Entrepreneurship has traditionally been viewed as inherently risky in the sense that there are no financial guarantees or promises of long-term security. For women, however, it can actually be less risky than the alternative—a life under someone else's dictum or working inside a structure that doesn't bring out their best. Many companies don't

LADIES WHO LAUNCH SURVEY

Are You Fulfilled with Your Business or Your Job?

	Lady Launchers:	Corporate Ladies:	Gentlemen Launchers:	Corporate Gentlemen:
Strongly Agree	68.1%	5.6%	68.4%	9.8%
Agree	26.3%	44.4%	23.7%	46.3%
Neutral	5.1%	18.5%	7.9%	19.5%
Disagree	0.5%	29.6%	0%	17.1%
Strongly Disagree	0%	1.9%	0%	7.3%

see "loyalty" as a mandatory offering anymore, and market conditions make it more about the bottom line than saving people from unemployment anyway. So, is entrepreneurship more high risk than corporate or nine-to-five life? Layoffs, adverse market conditions, and cutbacks can happen at any time, so security is more nebulous than it is certain. Entrepreneurship isn't a sure thing. But the mental, emotional, and physical risks of working in an environment that isn't suited to you may be the greatest danger of all.

These survey results speak for themselves. People in the launching categories are radically more fulfilled because, regardless of their level of success, they are building something important to them, something that stems from passion. Even if each of them is working eighteen-hour days, hasn't yet broken even, or can't go out to dinner with friends as often as she'd like, she is still significantly more fulfilled than her corporate sisters . . . and brothers.

Launchers are drastically more fulfilled for a number of reasons, which are highlighted in the next question we asked.

LADIES WHO LAUNCH SURVEY*

What Do You Like Most About Working for Yourself? (Select two.)

I love the freedom and flexibility.	49.1%
I feel more creative.	41.8%
It is more fulfilling.	30.2%
I like working hard and reaping the rewards.	28.4%
I love being my own boss.	24.3%
It allows me to spend more time with my kids.	14.5%
It is more fun.	7.9%

*Only the top results are listed.

Women are choosing entrepreneurship for lifestyle reasons and, most important, for the *freedom and flexibility, creativity,* and *fulfillment* that it brings. To further confirm our results we asked women in corporate jobs how much money they would trade for more freedom and flexibility in their lives.

LADIES WHO LAUNCH SURVEY

What Percentage of Your Income Would You Trade for the Ability to Design Your Own Life and Create Your Own Schedule . . . Work When You Want to Work?

	Corporate Ladies:
I like the structure of work and I wouldn't change anything.	9.4%
I wouldn't give up any money.	13.2%
10%	18.9%
20%	28.3%
30%	17.0%
40%	3.8%
50%	9.4%
More than 50%	0%

It is very telling that 77.4 percent of corporate women we surveyed would give up some amount of money for more freedom and flexibility. Launchers or entrepreneurs, especially women, are drawn to the opportunity to design a customized life, take charge of their destiny, and funnel projects or hobbies into profitable vessels. There is risk and there is pressure, yes. Office hours no longer exist, a seven-day workweek is common, expectations are much higher for entrepreneurs; you can never "skate" along and hope that the work gets done because you're the marketing, PR, customer service, and administration of your business. Entrepreneurship is hard, sometimes isolating, work. It's burdensome to answer to vendors, clients, creditors, and partners. There is often not a team in place to help make decisions, which means you are left to make them using any advisor you have (if you have one). At the end of the day, you say yes or no. That pressure can be very strenuous, to say nothing of the accountability; if it (or you) fails, it's on your watch and goes back to you. This also means it's your capital at risk. So, we don't have any notions that entrepreneurship is a walk in the park. It's more like a marathon with peaks and valleys, good days and hard days. But, the trade-off that many women and men are willing to accept is that they can spend more time with their children, work on their own hours (however long), go to yoga in the middle of the day, or have lunch with a friend without asking the boss for permission. You answer to no one but yourself and you can't get fired; there is no bureaucracy. This lifestyle also goes beyond the usual benefits of "freedom." The entrepreneurial lifestyle is a way to force yourself to look at what you really and truly want to do with yourself three to five to seven days a week. What it boils down to is that women are leaving corporate America or reshaping their presence in it for reasons wholly dependent on the lifestyle they want, and the career that complements that lifestyle.

Living Life with Your Own Style

By lifestyle we mean living your life by design; the whole enchilada, not just the part from nine to five. Here's one way to think about it: what if being out in the world was a seamless part of building your business? What if going to the grocery store was just as important as a trade show? What if the women from your yoga class were the same ones helping you launch a marketing strategy? To get a handle on launching as a lifestyle, think about this: everyone has friends who come from different parts or times of their lives. Imagine if you put these people together in the same room. Your friend with a dog-grooming business starts sending clients to another friend who owns a spa. A neighbor who designs Web sites partners with an old friend who writes them, and they go on vacations together and spend an hour each day brainstorming about the business. Because many women are natural connectors, this probably already happens for you organically. But we are talking about taking this to the next level and creating an entire life centered on connecting, launching, and living the bigger dream, without compromise. This doesn't necessarily mean excluding the corporate model, but it does mean pulling back a little bit, possibly reallocating time or energies, and shifting our perspectives.

LADIES WHO LAUNCH SURVEY

Entrepreneurs: Do You Work Harder Now That You Have Your Own Business?

	Lady Launchers:
Strongly Agree	52.1%
Agree	26.1%
Neutral	14.7%
Disagree	6.0%
Strongly Disagree	1.1%

LADIES WHO LAUNCH SURVEY

Entrepreneurs: Would You Choose Working Harder Over Working for Someone Else?

	Lady Launchers:
Strongly Agree	69.9%
Agree	22.6%
Neutral	5.8%
Disagree	1.6%
Strongly Disagree	.1%

There is an assumption that women are leaving corporate America because they don't want to work hard, they can't take it, they want a life of leisure, or their husbands, fathers, or other men are paying their way. We asked this question and here is what we discovered.

The survey responses make it clear that women are willing to work harder, but they want to work harder on their terms, on their own schedules, and as their own bosses. Women want control over the details of their day-to-day operations and they don't want to feel guilty for taking an afternoon off to run errands and maybe slip in a pedicure. They want to be able to go to the gym at 10 A.M., pick up a child at 3 P.M., send an e-mail at 9 P.M., or leave a voice mail at 2 A.M. Everyone can relate to the idea of there never being enough time in the day. What if we changed that paradigm? What if, while keeping deadlines and schedules in mind, we decided that the bigger lifestyle picture was more important as a whole, and kept this as a priority? Maybe women do best when they've taken care of their personal lives in the morning and are free to deliver their professional results in the afternoon. There is no one way for any woman to "do" her life. Each is different, which is why we encourage women to find their own rhythms whether they are in an office tower, in a boutique organization, or at a home office.

. . .

Portrait of a Lady

Hannah Sullivan, owner of Tahoe Trips & Trails, LLC, found herself burned-out from the high stress of the investment world and wanting more time to pursue her first love: outdoor excursions and adventure travel. After a successful but grueling career in the investment world, forty-year-old Hannah had built up enough personal equity to self-finance the purchase of Tahoe Trips & Trails, a business that would allow her to have the lifestyle she always dreamed of, incorporating her love of the outdoors with a moneymaking opportunity. Tahoe Trips & Trails offers active travel adventures for individuals and groups in scenic areas such as California's Lake Tahoe, the Northern California coast, the California wine country, Yosemite National Park, southern Utah, and Jackson Hole,

Wyoming. Some of the trips are all about hiking, while others are multisport agen-das that include a combination of hiking, biking, white-water rafting, and kayak-ing tours guided by experts who love the outdoors. Travelers enjoy gourmet food and spend evenings in the comfort of inns chosen for their luxury and character. Although Hannah admittedly works incredibly hard, owning her own company al-lows her more time to pursue her personal athletic interests, and to fulfill her dream of giving back and connecting with her community through teaching skiing to dis-abled kids and giving away trips to local charities.

To illustrate this lifestyle conversation more clearly, the following is an example of a nonlaunching lifestyle compared to one that illus-trates launching. In this model, the launching woman in the second example could be a business owner or a corporate employee. It's so important to understand that our argument is not that everyone should leap into entrepreneurship, as defined literally as the act of "starting one's own business." But tapping into your own inner entrepreneur is a way of life that can be applied to a multitude of circumstances.

A Nonlaunching Life

7 A.M.: Get up, get ready, rush to work. Eat bagel and drink coffee in the car.

9 A.M.: At desk, answering e-mails, starting the day.

Noon: Lunch at desk.

3 P.M.: Staff meeting. Tired and feeling lethargic, but meeting is obligatory. Coffee pick-me-up.

6 P.M.: Start to wrap up the day.

7 P.M.: Rush to the gym for a quick workout (if you don't have kids). Running home to be with kids before bed if you do have kids.

8 P.M.: Meet friends for dinner or family dinner at home.

10 P.M.: TV for an hour.

11 P.M.: Bedtime.

Repeat . . .

A Launching Life

7 A.M.: Get up, take time to eat, spend time with your kids (if you have them), meditate, stretch, read the paper, write in a journal, go for a run

or walk, sip coffee, pet the cat, walk the dog. Pick up new bestseller at local bookstore, and run into old friend who just moved back to town. Set up lunch date.

10 A.M.: At work. Check e-mail, dive into work with gusto.

12:30 P.M.: Lunch. Meet husband/boyfriend/girlfriend for lunch at favorite sushi joint. Browse a couple of stores afterward for creative ideas.

2 P.M.: Staff meeting. Some great ideas have danced through your head. An idea hit you while in one of the boutiques, and you introduce it to the team.

3 P.M.: Return calls, e-mail, project management.

3:45 P.M.: Spend time with kids (if you have them) when they get home from school.

4:30 P.M.: From home, create strategy with team to implement plan. Return e-mails.

6:30 P.M.: Pottery class.

7:45 P.M.: Drink and light dinner with leader of local nonprofit who needs your corporate support, and who is also someone you fantasize about working with full time. Calls returned to and from dinner.

9:30 P.M.: Home. Long, juicy chat with mom/dad/sister/friend far away.

10 P.M.: Answer e-mails

11 P.M.: Watch Jon Stewart or maybe read *Vogue*. Fun story on dressing from the forties. Note to self about new vintage boutique around the corner.

Sleep!

The difference between designing your own life and being a slave to it is vast. Women come to Ladies Who Launch facing the struggle between what society expects and what they themselves really desire. Often our true desires are so repressed that we simply feel emotional, confused, and out of touch. We are good girls and we have been taught our whole lives to follow the rules. Unfortunately, following the rules hasn't made us happy. Women are yearning to escape from this confining structure. We've been told we can't have it all, so we might as well choose what it is we really want and be prepared to sacrifice everything else. The Ladies Who Launch Incubator, which we'll describe in more detail in Part II of this book, is our answer to the issue. The Incubator was designed to offer a safe environment in which to express these emotions and explore alternative possibilities. Women who have either not listened to themselves early enough or had terrible corporate experiences have called the Ladies Who Launch Incubator a "corporate recovery program"—a place where they can find validation for their feelings and the support, encouragement, and information they need to design a life of their own. Others just see it as a way of exploring their life outside of a fixed job that they may be totally content to keep. The Incubator is just another tool in the shed, and you can't have too many of those.

. . .

Portrait of a Lady

Carrie Simon was doing better than well in her hedge fund sales job; she had followed the path everyone expected from her and rose through the corporate ranks to great success. When she became burned-out she felt bad and guilty about not being happy. After all, she had a highly coveted job and she was doing well; so many people would have traded anything to be in her position. She came to the Ladies Who Launch Incubator and gained the courage to leave her job without knowing what she was going to do next. One of her greatest challenges was learning to adjust to living without structure, and to having moments in the day when she wasn't being "productive." She is taking time off to explore and investigate a path that is of her own making and figuring out what she can do in her work life that is both challenging and fulfilling.

Mommy Launchers

A New York Times front-page article reported in 2005 that women at Ivy League schools are planning to quit their jobs in their thirties and have children. A 2003 New York Times Magazine article indicated that highly educated women are choosing to stay at home with their children due to the stress of dual-income-earner circumstances (long hours and lots of travel). Both articles cite anecdotal evidence that women are increasingly opting out of employment when they have children. The truth is there is absolutely no economic data to support these stories. In fact, according to the Bureau of Labor Statistics, in 2004 (the latest year for which we have a full year of data), the reports show that having children at home actually increased women's participation in the labor force compared to prior years. We asked our mothers in the Ladies Who Launch community (admittedly a bit biased toward entrepreneurship) if they had left the workforce after having a child (or children), and if and how they planned on reentering the workforce.

LADIES WHO LAUNCH SURVEY

Do You Plan on Reentering the Workforce After Having Children?

I plan to get a full-time job doing what I was doing before.	2.4%
I plan to get a full-time job doing something different than what I did before.	7.3%
I plan to work part-time.	9.8%
I plan to do what I was doing on a freelance or consulting basis.	4.9%
I plan to launch my own business.	39%
I am not ever going back to work.	0%
I would go back to work, but only if it were something I was passionate about.	19.5%
I would go back to work, but only if it gave me complete flexibility over my life.	17.1%

The women we surveyed all plan to go back to work doing something, but very few are planning to get a full-time job doing what they were doing before the birth of their child. They might stay home for a year or two and then enter the world with a new force of creativity and motivation. The conversion rate of women leaving the workforce to

raise children and then reentering it to start businesses or work freelance or as a consultant is pretty high.

. . .

Portrait of a Lady

Molly Snyder, founder of Metropolitan Moms, left the traditional investment banking world to analyze businesses being considered for the receipt
of monies from the September 11th Fund (not strictly limited to entrepreneurs).
She absolutely loved what she was doing and the path she was on; in fact this was
her dream job. However her departure from the traditional corporate world of
investment banking to a world that focused on entrepreneurial businesses did not
change the fact that she remained in a traditional work environment that was not
as flexible as she preferred. When she and her husband decided to start a family,
she had nine months of pregnancy to realize that regardless of her passion for the
work, the hours would be unsustainable for her in the long term. She did not want
to go back to work five days a week and even a part-time four-day schedule did
not offer her the flexibility she craved upon entering the world of motherhood. Yet
staying at home full time, while financially possible, seemed untenable as well.
She craved intellectual stimulation, a purpose, and the chance to be creative and
make things happen while still retaining the flexibility that allowed her maximum
time with her children. In connecting with other moms, she found that many were
not satisfied with the traditional playgroups where moms would get together and
discuss the latest diaper-changing fiasco or the newest stroller on the market. She
saw a need that was not being met and asked herself how she could incorporate her
baby girl into a creative and intellectually challenging life that suited her. She
found the answer by creating Metropolitan Moms, an organization that offers
museum visits, gallery walks, culinary adventures, and neighborhood explo-
rations for moms, babies, and toddlers. Not only does she tote her toddler to Metropolitan Moms classes during off-school hours, but she has created a life to fit
the mommy lifestyle. She always picks her daughter up from school and she works
around activities that she values doing with her daughter. She may not work at all
one day, then work six hours one night after putting her daughter to bed. She is
focused on strategically growing the business and expanding it to new cities. She
says, "To some extent, this business would probably be growing so much faster if I

did not have children. I know I have to be patient. My partner and I turn down opportunities every day and try to focus on those that are optimal for our business right now. I have no regrets."

The Ladies Who Launch Way

Let's give you the bottom line about launching as a way of life. The Ladies Who Launch way celebrates creativity and entrepreneurship in any shape or form, as long as a woman feels inspired, interested in her life, and wants to keep it moving forward in new and interesting ways. It also prioritizes a way of life that includes more flexibility and creativity with a splash of lifestyle. This is what feels good to women, and what allows us to perform at our highest levels.

Launchwork

Design your life. We are all given the same amount of time in a day, a week, a year. The question is, what are we going to do with this time and life that we were given? With that in mind, the Ladies Who Launch way encourages women to take control and find original ways to design their lives to really flow and to embrace their multidimensional interests. These lives take some planning and a conscious effort to see where you're going before you end up burned-out at the end of a long road. To start, let's find out how much of your life is created versus how much of it is reactionary, or simply meeting the demands put forth by others. What do you have and what do you need, and are those two essentials matched up with each other?

Take a moment to make a short list of the top five things that are important to you. For example:

1. Time with family
2. Success in my work
3. Connections with friends

4. Travel and adventure
5. Health and taking care of myself

Make your own list and then look at your date book from last week and see if any of your priorities are present in the way you spent your time. Did you eat dinner with your family? Did you have fun at work and find a sense of moving forward doing something you love? Did you have lunch with a friend? Did you think about where you want to go on your next vacation and share that with your significant other or a friend? Did you take a Pilates class? It may sound clinical, but it takes some designing, crafting, and discipline to have a balanced life that "has it all."

Now, put one thing in your calendar for each of the five areas this week. For example:

1. Plan a picnic with the family
2. Start a blog
3. Make a date to meet a friend for tea
4. Spend some time on the Internet researching vacations in Costa Rica
5. Register for a belly-dancing class

Design your ideal day. With no thought of "income," answer the question "What would you be doing if you had more flexibility?" What would your day look like? Do what you need to do, take a day off work or book a babysitter, and try and live that life, close to your ideal, for at least one day.

Create a "life book." When interior designers, fashion designers, or art directors are looking for inspiration, they sometimes start with images torn from magazines that represent an overall feeling for what they are going to try to create, the vibe they're looking to channel. Start your own life book (or it could be a bulletin board, a box, or you could simply start pasting things into your launch journal). This is a visual diary of sorts that collects a sense of what you would like your life to look like. It shows the universe what you are thinking about in your head. Ours has magazine cutouts of houses we would love to live in, of men who look like good husbands, of careers, jewelry we hope to own or borrow, places we would like to visit, women we admire, activities we want to do with our children. The life book becomes a scrapbook and a reminder of everything we want to be. Start this book now, but think of it as an open-ended project that keeps growing as you keep growing. Begin yours with a statement about what is important to you in your life. It can be an organic, simple phrase, for example:

Balance and aesthetic beauty and comfort are the hallmarks of good life.

My greatest loves are my family and doing something I love every day.

My passion is my work as a painter. Travel, interesting strangers, and unique experiences feed this work.

My life is a mystery to me, and letting it unfold organically is the most exciting thing I can imagine.

My mind is my greatest asset. I want to continue to cultivate it with a partner, in my work, in my physical body, and in my spiritual life.

RECOMMENDED BOOKS

The Creative Habit by Twyla Tharp. This celebrated choreographer has written one of the best books on creating and channeling creativity in your life. Easy to read, easier to digest, she gives morsels of her own life that can apply to anyone—whether in a suit or wearing ballet slippers.

Design Your Self by Karim Rashid. Industrial designers know a thing or two about living in style, and Rashid serves up au courant courses in living well, eating right, being in relationships, and more.

RECOMMENDED MOVIE

Baby Boom. This little gem is straight out of the eighties, with shoulderpads and all. Diane Keaton is a Lady Who Launches, and so is her character. Watch how she takes the reins, changes her life, and becomes far more successful than she could have ever hoped to be inside the walls of her Manhattan office.

3

·········

Women, the Natural Connectors

It probably won't surprise you to learn that women are biologically programmed to connect; their happiness and livelihood depend on it. Have you ever heard the expression "The people make the place"? This is especially true for women, who thrive when there are other like-minded people around them. A woman could land the most coveted, well-paid job in her company but still not find it very satisfying without a cool friend to grab coffee with or the opportunity to chat with someone who also reads the Sunday Styles section of the *New York Times,* to say nothing of finding a fun person to collaborate with. She could also live in the chicest neighborhood, with the prettiest yard and the most wonderful local restaurants, but without other treasured people in her universe, her life and home simply aren't as lively. The converse is also true. Dispatch a woman to a dingy airport, remote bus terminal, or foreign classroom, and if she can find someone to connect with she will be happy. Women can bond over something as small as a love for orchids, organic food, hiking, or English Breakfast tea. While men appreciate having things in common with other men, if two women have a business meeting and realize they both have a weakness for Jimmy Choo shoes, something changes in their business relationship. Women look for common ground in order to build a community. They want to connect on more than one level, and it doesn't dilute the business relationship, it makes it stronger. The camaraderie, support, and the female intuitive quality have been cited by happy, successful Ladies Who Launch as the secret weapons and a common characteristics of their rich and rewarding lives.

Malcolm Gladwell's book *The Tipping Point* defines a connector as someone who both knows lots of people and who also has an extraordinary knack for making friends and acquaintances. Many women have these qualities; they just don't realize it or see it as one of their most valuable attributes. On the other hand, many women, especially those in jobs or roles whose success depends on connections (real estate, sales of any kind, fund-raising, development), use connector skills all the time. Being a connector means things come to you more easily and that you have "reach" in many different circles. Someone's child needs a good tutor? You know one. Someone else needs an honest mechanic? No problem. From the mundane, everyday connections to the bigger, more life-changing ones, being a connector can only serve you well! We say that women are inherently connectors; it is inbred in our DNA. So the question isn't, "Are you a connector?" the question is, "Are you fully using and taking advantage of your connector ability?" Here is another quiz (remember, no grades) designed to help you find out if you are truly leveraging your own natural resource.

LADIES WHO LAUNCH SURVEY

Are You Stuck in the Traditional Model?

The traditional business model requires gathering hierarchical power and using vertical relationships to get to the top (think Michael Douglas in *Wall Street*). Horizontal relationships, equally as powerful but more feminine (think Melanie Griffith in *Working Girl*), are inclusive and encourage partnerships. What does that mean? One is more interested in being alone at the top and gathering power. The other is interested in including others in success and using collaborations as a way to get there.

I actively seek environments or social situations outside of my
family unit or childhood friends circle.   ___Yes ___No

I like to partner and collaborate on projects.   ___Yes ___No

I am more likely to talk about possibilities than complain with
my friends. Be honest!   ___Yes ___No

When I like a product or service, I tell everyone I know.   ___Yes ___No

I enjoy meeting and getting to know people for the pure sake
of talking to someone new, without an agenda.   ___Yes ___No

I often think of putting one person in touch with another when
I think they could benefit in some way.   ___Yes ___No

I love throwing and/or going to parties, even if they involve
people I don't yet know.   ___Yes ___No

The people around me are a diverse mix of motivated and
creative people.   ___Yes ___No

I feel great (not guilty) when I am having lunch with a friend
in the middle of a busy day and consider that productive.   ___Yes ___No

I enjoy spending time alone in order to recharge.   ___Yes ___No

I get creative ideas and business epiphanies from the people
in my life.   ___Yes ___No

I have more than two hundred people in my contact list
or address book.   ___Yes ___No

While getting a manicure in my local salon, I often chat with
the other women around me.   ___Yes ___No

When a friend needs help with something, I go out of my
way to connect her with the right person, even if I don't
know that person very well.   ___Yes ___No

When I have to call someone I don't know, I feel excited
to see where it could lead.   ___Yes ___No

I find it easy to make long-standing friendships.   ___Yes ___No

I initiate invitations to people I only know tangentially
(people I know through others but not at all well).   ___Yes ___No

When I look at my address book (online or hard-backed)
it contains names of people I knew years ago,
in addition to newer acquaintances.   ___Yes ___No

If you answered no to five or more questions, it could mean one of two things:

1. You're an introvert and like it that way (in which case we can only present the options that being more expansive might give you).

2. You could be more inclusive of others in your life, introvert or not, in ways that would add more creativity, more connection, and more excitement than you currently have.

These questions are meant to illuminate the difference between building outward (connecting with people who live not only in your professional world but also in circles outside of it) and connecting only with those who line the path on your way somewhere else. If your answers tended toward your being an easy friend to even those you don't know well initially, and you have a proclivity for staying friends with people for many years, you are definitely a connector. If your answers indicated inclusiveness, you are leveraging your natural connecting skills (Brava!). You are probably one or two degrees of separation away from anyone you want to get to in your city and perhaps the world. If you are in the "five or more" category, you may not be using your internal connecting device because you haven't realized the potential benefits. Laziness, snobbery, shyness, or introversion may also keep you from being open, but it doesn't mean that you are *not* a connector. Plus, there's always room for everyone to be more of what they already are.

Connecting is a critical component of launching. You have countless abilities that bring people together for mutual benefit, and even more skills that will bring you work, relationships, friends, social events, and so forth. One very wise friend, who happens to be a man and oversees an educational fund for women in Third World countries, says "Educate a man, educate one person. Educate a woman, educate a community." To explain why giving a woman an education pays higher dividends than giving one to a man: women pass along, include, and broaden what they're given to their children, sisters, friends, and colleagues. Having more friends doesn't mean having a better life, it only means that being connected gives you more options and that you have the ability to make more happen.

When we were shopping our book to different publishers, one of the senior editors at a publishing house we were visiting said, "In all the years I have been here I have never had two men come in together to pitch a book, but it happens all the time with women." While we remain sure that male writing partners exist (there are many examples of men creating very successful partnerships), we see this book partnership as a reflection of women being more naturally inclined for collaboration on every level. We love it, we seek it, and we thrive on it.

Hanging Out to Move It Forward

Plenty of women get together for coffee, over playdates for their kids, or for no other reason than to have fun, but most women say that they don't do it enough. To ensure connecting, women have always created ways to come together to move forward. Your grandmother may have connected over canasta or quilting. Your mother was or is probably part of a walking group, or a book or bridge club. These days, women run together, meditate together, travel together, or meet over knitting circles because they want to connect, but also because they do better at accomplishing goals among other women.

How many times have you gotten together with a group of women and come away with a new doctor referral, the source for a pair of shoes you must have, a recipe you want to try, or that revolutionary business idea you feel compelled to start? Everything from the Junior League, the Girl Scouts, investment clubs, and quilting and book clubs serve the purpose of bringing women together. We have heard from many of our Ladies Who Launch that the corporate structure, with its daily routine of going to the office every day, serves this community-building function. We started Ladies Who Launch to give women a community through different outlets: through online inspiration, message boards, and a network, through our in-person Incubator programs, events, and PR opportunities. Ladies Who Launch is an example of a new approach to creating community, connecting women through creativity, motivation, and lifestyle; using technology to cross national and international borders, age ranges, ethnicities, industries, and socioeconomic levels. If you've ever moved to a new city or changed jobs, you suddenly appreciate the familiarity of your old neighborhood and the sense of safety and happiness underlying your day-to-day activities. Your girlfriends, now farther away, aren't there to meet you at the corner for coffee or take you home after Lasik surgery. That sense of sisterhood and support that emotionally carries you is gone, and although it doesn't mean you'll freeze to death in winter or be left behind to die in the desert like hundreds of years ago, it does mean you aren't quite operating at your best and could even suffer from low-grade depression. For virtually all women companionship and female community are not an option, but a necessity. Being a connector widens your circle of community, with both men and women, and the time you spend socializing is good. If you've held back from being social because it isn't "on track" with your professional goals, you might need to question that belief.

LADIES WHO LAUNCH SURVEY

I Am a Connector, I Love Putting People in Touch with Each Other
When I Feel That They Could Benefit in Some Way:

	Featured Ladies:	Launching Ladies:	Corporate Ladies:	Launching Gentlemen:	Corporate Gentlemen:
Strongly Agree	58.1%	52.7%	30.7%	42.3%	20.7%
Agree	38.7%	33.1%	46.6%	40.4%	41.4%
Neutral	3.2%	11.4%	18.7%	15.4%	24.1%
Disagree	0%	2.5%	4.0%	1.9%	13.8%
Strongly Disagree	0%	.3%	0%	0%	0%

More than half of the launching women polled described themselves as connectors, and the majority of all women polled agreed that they are connectors. The featured ladies *know* they are connectors; as you can see on the preceding page, not a single one disagreed. Launchers feel that they are stronger connectors, which makes sense, because their livelihood depends on it. Essentially, these results support the concept that women are natural connectors and that these connections have proven successful in achieving personal and professional goals.

LADIES WHO LAUNCH SURVEY

I Get Creative Ideas and Business Epiphanies from the People in My Life:

	Featured Ladies:	Launching Ladies:	Corporate Ladies:	Launching Gentlemen:	Corporate Gentlemen:
Strongly Agree	48.4%	40.6%	18.7%	32.0%	13.8%
Agree	38.7%	43.3%	50.6%	40.0%	58.6%
Neutral	9.7%	12.4%	20.0%	24.0%	20.7%
Disagree	3.2%	3.1%	10.7%	2.0%	6.9%
Strongly Disagree	0%	.6%	0%	2.0%	0%

Featured Ladies credit the people in their lives with much of their creative energy and ensuing success. Corporate women also draw on others for creative inspiration but are, perhaps, constrained by their corporate environment.

We have discovered that the traditional business philosophy is either in direct conflict with feminine tendencies of acting on intuition or connection with others, or has no relation to it and feels very unnatural for women. For example, telling a woman that upon conception of her entrepreneurial idea she needs to write a business plan immediately, work out all the numbers, and define her exit strategy is counterintuitive and counterproductive to her natural tendency to go out in the world and connect. More typically she would get information and hash through a plan slowly by bouncing ideas off those around her. She'd prefer to set up meetings with people working in her area of interest, get information from friends and colleagues, or enjoy a long dinner and glass of wine from which a potential or unexpected partnership might arise.

Society relentlessly encourages productivity, usually defined by how many clients you have, how many pages you've written, or how many hours you work, but that quantified work ethic does not celebrate women, or anyone for that matter, getting together. Parties are viewed as "playtime"—the opposite of work. Spending time with our children is cavalierly referred to as "mentally unstimulating." Social interaction is often considered leisurely or frivolous when it actually *is* productive, especially for women. Women are more likely to have a creative idea when out in the world circulating or even having lunch with a friend, rather than buried in paperwork at a desk. This is why you see many women entrepreneurs create products that they developed out of their personal needs. Their ideas come while pushing strollers, socializing at a party with a friend-who-knows-a-friend, driving from one meeting to the next, or quite simply just being in the moment. These ideas come either from frustration or a strong desire to have something they aren't able to find on the market. In many cases, the money part is secondary. This is why it's so difficult for women to switch gears and go from the ideation stage to the hunched-over-a-business-plan stage. This means often being alone, calculator in one hand, extra-strong coffee in the other. Life can feel like it's on hold, even though what a business plan is supposed to do is "plan" for a future endeavor. We don't begrudge the business plan (and we'll talk about it more in chapter 5), we're simply pointing out that it can feel like an abrupt end to what was fun and creative. Suddenly it's all about projections and estimates, cash flow, and profit and loss. Business plans are useful, but because developing a business concept using social networks is not celebrated in society, many women feel guilty and wrong for going against the standard formula of writing one. We feel unproductive or worse, stupid, when we are actually being the most productive by doing what is natural and fun. When something is fun it is generally assumed that it can't be productive or materially worthwhile. People associate blood, sweat, and tears with success, when in reality, there's a lot to learn about the road to success when it is paved with pleasure and connecting. How many times have you made an introduction that led to a lifelong friendship, or became a source of information that would have taken someone else hours of research in isolation to understand? It is simply much more enjoyable for women to move forward through and with others! It means not feeling alone, and using this community as a focus group, sounding board, or a human LexisNexis. The group taps into many other resources, and to discount its importance is misguided.

LADIES WHO LAUNCH SURVEY

Do You Have a Supportive Team Around You?
Team _____ (insert your name here)

	Featured Ladies:	Launching Ladies:	Corporate Ladies:	Launching Gentlemen:	Corporate Gentlemen:
Strongly Agree	64.5%	46.3%	36.0%	39.2%	34.5%
Agree	25.8%	39.1%	52.0%	51.0%	55.2%
Neutral	6.5%	11.8%	6.7%	3.9%	10.3%
Disagree	3.2%	2.3%	5.3%	3.9%	0%
Strongly Disagree	0%	.5%	0%	2.0%	0%

When you consider the formula for success, our Featured Ladies are pioneering the way. They understand the value and importance of having a supportive team around them, and not just as it relates to their work. A support team could be everything from family and friends to hired assistants, cleaning ladies, babysitters, chiropractors, yoga instructors, and hair colorists. Connecting with a team helps keep you moving and productive; they have your back, they are people you can rely on, and they make your life better in some way. Most women we know have some type of well-being team; the acupuncturist, the therapist, the mystic, the healer, the trainer, yoga instructor, facialist, waxer, and manicurist, to offer a few examples. Many of us feel paralyzed about launching anything because we feel overwhelmed by the perception of the work and struggle we associate with taking on a new venture rather than anticipating the joy that comes with perceiving our launch projects as expressions of our creative selves. The team we create is a resource for coping with this overwhelming feeling. What we can learn from our featured ladies is of critical importance. To have a supportive team around you means not only the nonnegotiable players (supportive spouses, partners, and friends), but also a team of positive, contributing members, assembled by you, to add their unique value to your life. It is natural for us to want support, but many of us (so busy producing) forget the importance of spending the time to build the support network that will lead to more success, in every dimension.

Essentially, our message is "be yourself" and the opportunities will come. We are telling you to do what comes naturally, to build strong relationships, and to stop suffering. Stop believing that success means sacrifice. Sometimes this means slowing down to look around and check in with what feels good versus what is expected of you. Take inventory of where you are and where you want to be and build a team to get you there. While reading this, did you feel an unexpected stroke of creative genius? Has something you never thought of before come to mind? Did an obvious person you should meet with surface in your thoughts? Is there a connection you could make by e-mail or phone that might lead to something else? These thoughts may provoke more uncertainty but doesn't it feel also exciting? What we are trying to do is to get you back to your natural and feminine state of "connectedness" because we know that everything will flow from there.

LADIES WHO LAUNCH SURVEY

I Have This Number of People in My Contact List, Both Personal and Professional:

	Featured Ladies:	Launching Ladies:	Corporate Ladies:	Launching Gentlemen:	Corporate Gentlemen:
Less than 100	5.7%	27.3%	35.1%	13.5%	21.4%
100–250	22.9%	27.6%	33.8%	25.0%	35.7%
250–500	20%	18.9%	17.6%	21.2%	35.7%
500–1,000	20%	13.8%	8.1%	19.2%	3.6%
1,000 or More	31.4%	12.4%	5.4%	21.1%	3.6%

We define our successful Featured Ladies as those who are balancing their lifestyle while launching. Connections and success are the equivalent of a happily married couple. Without connections (togetherness) you couldn't very easily build anything, and without success (an inherent sense of happiness alone or together) you'd have no measure of your connections. The Featured Ladies are significantly more connected, with 31.4 percent saying that they have more than one thousand contacts. Whether they had great connections to get where they landed or it happened as a result of pursuing their dream, they collected barrels of contacts, they are master connectors, and they acknowledge this as the sweet spot in their lives.

Knowing many people helps you grow and expand your projects. It isn't just so that you get more holiday cards, have more people to e-mail, or invite to brunch, it's also a way to spread the word on anything from where you went on vacation to a new shampoo that makes your hair shinier to your cell phone service or a babysitter. Women are the best natural marketers around and women definitely understand this better than men.

LADIES WHO LAUNCH SURVEY

Word-of-Mouth Has Been an Important Part of Building My Business:

	Featured Ladies:	Launching Ladies:	Launching Gentlemen:
Strongly Agree	75%	70.9%	67.3%
Agree	17.9%	22.8%	23.1%
Neutral	7.1%	5.5%	5.8%
Disagree	0%	.8%	3.8%
Strongly Disagree	0%	0%	0%

Our ladies credit word-of-mouth as the muscle behind their marketing strategy. They know what advertisers and marketers have zeroed in on ages ago. Women are far more likely to express their emotions and feelings about their preferences for all kinds of products and services and share them with their friends. Any multilevel marketing model employs this concept! Avon and Mary Kay have become multimillion-dollar businesses based on this. This power spreads good news *and* bad. A woman who receives bad customer service or a poorly performing tube of mascara is much more likely than a man (who has an equivalent interaction) to spread the word. A woman won't shut up about it! When Featured Lady Patsy Aiken started Chez Ami home parties to sell her children's clothing designs, her business grew by nearly 30 percent as compared with her wholesale business. That's because when women connect to socialize and to shop, they create a viral impact that is unparalleled and great for business.

. . .

Portrait of a Lady

Smita Paul, founder of Indigo Handloom, launched her business because of a lifelong passion for Indian textiles. A journalist by trade, she discovered the unique qualities of handwoven cloth from India while writing a story about the Indian silk industry. Smita launched Indigo Handloom in 2003 with the dual goal of wanting to expose and bring these beautiful items to the United States as well as provide jobs and income to the people of a specific Indian community who were skilled at producing these pieces. She started producing these beautiful handwoven shawls and founded Indigo Handloom in 2003. When Smita started marketing these incredibly beautiful shawls, she became very frustrated, realizing that the process of selling to stores was completely unenjoyable and energy-draining for her. She preferred to focus on the creative design of the shawls and connecting with the Indian artisans. She so loathed pitching to buyers that she decided to create an alternate way of selling her beautiful pieces: "Good Karma Parties." To start, Smita found a hostess whose greatest joy was organizing parties. She gave her a budget for food and wine, free products, and also donated a percentage of sales to the hostess's favorite charity. Smita was able to sell in a way that suited her personality and created an additional revenue stream, and she has become so successful that there are "Good Karma Parties" every month. In this scenario, everyone wins.

Smita's story speaks not only to her desire to connect with other women in a fun and original way, but also to her need to connect with the world, give back to the Indian community, and provide opportunities for women in the United States to earn a part-time income while maintaining a flexible lifestyle.

Many marketing experts cite viral marketing as the key ingredient in profiling brands whose popularity has soared. *Daily Candy* and Baby Einstein grew quickly in short time periods, with little or no traditional advertising, based solely on the word-of-mouth buzz that their primarily female markets created. Baby Einstein sold to Disney for $25 million in 2001. *Daily Candy* has amassed more than a million subscribers, with new ones signing up at a quick clip. People talking to one another, and lots of them doing it, creates a swell. Gladwell said it

LADIES WHO LAUNCH SURVEY

When I Like a Product or Service I Tell Everyone I Know:

	Ladies:	Gentlemen:
Frequently	55.9%	28.7%
Often	33.3%	40.4%
Sometimes	10.0%	26.5%
Seldom	.8%	4.4%
Never	0%	0%

When I Am Disappointed in a Product or Service, I Tell Everyone I Know:

	Ladies:	Gentlemen:
Frequently	35.3%	22.8%
Often	34.2%	41.2%
Sometimes	27.3%	33.8%
Seldom	3.1%	1.5%
Never	0.1%	0.7%

best in *The Tipping Point* when he talked about the contagiousness of emotions: "Some of us, after all, are very good at expressing emotions and feelings, which means that we are far more emotionally contagious than the rest of us."

. . .

Portrait of a Lady

When Julie Aigner Clark launched the Baby Einstein Company in 1997, she had no idea that in the first year of operation her company would make $100K in revenue without any advertising whatsoever. Julie was simply trying to create a product she was unable to find for her own baby. Her passion, enthusiasm, and innovation are what drove this project forward despite limited resources. As Julie recounts, "The first Baby Einstein video took off because it was a completely new concept. It was an entirely new idea. No one else had videos for babies. During the first five and a half years, we never ran an ad. The videos made babies happy. Parents told their friends. News articles and publicity opportunities came to us." Ultimately she sold Baby Einstein to Disney for $25 million, and now she is on to her next project, Safe Side, which provides DVDs that teach kids about stranger and Internet safety.

It is amazing how profitable a little chitchat can be. There are many other stories that drive home the same point. The power of the spoken word can bring you to the basement or take you to the penthouse.

. . .

Portrait of a Lady

To earn enough money to open a glass studio in New York, Heather Moore, founder of Heather Moore Jewelry, started making and selling jewelry using sterling silver and glass enamel. Through word-of-mouth communications and friends donning her creations, the jewelry quickly took off and today Heather is the owner and designer of Heather Moore Jewelry, which creates one-of-a-kind necklaces, rings, earrings, bracelets, and holiday ornaments from sterling silver, eighteen-carat gold, and glass enamel. Her wearable works of art have been featured in many magazines, including Lucky, InStyle, Real Simple, Elle.com, Accessories, Elle, Freudian, Women's Wear Daily, Mademoiselle, Talk, and Child. After her initial business took off, she went through a phase of feeling uninspired and stuck: "Once *you get through the learning curve of your business, no matter how seemingly creative, you have to re-create in order to stay fulfilled and inspired. What I found is that it never gets easy to put myself out there creatively, every time I try something new I worry about the reaction of my customers, but it is the only way to find true fulfillment in business and in life."* As a present to herself, Heather created a personalized keepsake necklace containing a chain with dangling semi-precious stones and coinlike charms hanging off the chain containing the names of her children and husband engraved in an almost scribbled handwritten style. She began wearing it and suddenly everyone (including us) was asking her to create one for them. She could not believe that she had stumbled upon the next big thing in her business simply by being passionate and creative for herself. It has led to powerful word-of-mouth and a demand she can hardly keep up with!

We have heard over and over again from our Ladies that one of the greatest gifts to women for both connecting and launching is technology. Technology allows women the freedom and flexibility to do so much more and connect whenever and wherever they like. Whether it is the ubiquitous cell phone or the Internet, these forms of connecting are the dear and treasured friends of women.

While technology is a friend to the world, women benefit perhaps

LADIES WHO LAUNCH SURVEY

I Own the Following:

	Featured Ladies:	Launching Ladies:	Corporate Ladies:	Launching Gentlemen:	Corporate Gentlemen:
Laptop computer	82.8%	76.6%	78.4%	88.5%	86.2%
PDF device such as a BlackBerry, Treo, or other	37.9%	34.2%	50.0%	55.8%	51.7%
Wireless networking	62.1%	64.4%	67.6%	78.8%	62.1%

LADIES WHO LAUNCH SURVEY

I Use the Internet for the Following Purposes (Choose All That Apply):

	Featured Ladies:	Launching Ladies:	Corporate Ladies:	Launching Gentlemen:	Corporate Gentlemen:
Get information/ research	96.7%	99.9%	100%	100%	96.6%
Shop for products and services	93.3%	95.7%	94.6%	96.2%	93.1%
E-mail/Corre-spondence	100%	99.2%	97.3%	98.1%	100%
Networking sites	36.7%	49%	27.0%	30.8%	10.3%
Sort pictures or video	43.3%	42.4%	59.5%	40.4%	44.8%
Manage my Web site, either personal or business	83.3%	79.1%	25.7%	51.9%	34.5%
Blogging	26.7%	19.3%	8.1%	11.5%	24.1%
Podcasting or music downloads	30%	30.8%	43.2%	38.5%	37.9%

more from it than men, simply because it gives them a greater amount of the freedom, flexibility, and connection that they crave. Technology has built a bridge between us that doesn't require time-consuming in-person meetings and allows people to send a message to check on a friend with the flu, or e-mail from a fabric expedition to India. Any woman not fully taking advantage of this modern wonder is missing out as badly as if she forgot the Nordstrom shoe sale! Technology is simply another vehicle for connecting, and it allows us to do it faster, more efficiently, and from anywhere.

LADIES WHO LAUNCH SURVEY

I Spend This Amount of Time on the Internet:

	Featured Ladies:	Launching Ladies:	Corporate Ladies:	Launching Gentlemen:	Corporate Gentlemen:
1-5 Hours Per Week	6.7%	9.6%	13.7%	5.8%	3.4%
5-10 Hours Per Week	13.3%	19.1%	27.4%	26.8%	24.1%
10-15 Hours Per Week	13.3%	18%	13.7%	21.2%	31.1%
More than 15 Hours Per Week	66.7%	53.3%	45.2%	46.2%	41.4%

Ladies and gentlemen are networking online, managing their Web sites, conducting research, and communicating.

Launchwork

These exercises are designed to link your natural talent for reaching out to others with a focused ability called connecting. Connectors aren't being cheeky when they say they have the world at their fingertips. They really do. What you want to do is look at your life and think about who is either a gateway to people you might want to know or an outgoing person who seems to just have friends in interesting places. This isn't about opportunism in its crudest form; this is about letting people into your life. We can all "use" each other and we all want to be "used." Using is good; it just gets a bad name because it's articulated in the context of not being appreciative, not having honest intentions, or not being genuine. This is the antithesis of that! Here is an example of Amy's from when she first moved to L.A. She wanted to meet people and expand her network, but didn't know where to start.

So she made a list of everyone she thought was interesting or fun, and made an effort to have lunch or coffee with them, invite them to events she attended, introduce them to her boyfriend (now husband), Josh, and so on.

The Social Audit

Leigh: wife of Josh's friend, works for Yahoo
Rebecca: wife of Josh's friend, freelance visual researcher
Henri: Independent film producer
Sarah: Handbag designer, Simply Sarah
Kathy: Author and wife of old friend/contact
Lysa: Fashion stylist, friend of a friend from New York
Jane: Executive and friend of an advertising mogul in New York
Martin: Actor
Nick: Writer

And so on . . .

This will help you see who is on your radar and how to expand your world. Sometimes it takes writing it down to make it happen! This list will by no means represent every person you know. It's meant to illustrate people you already like and know well, and provide jumping-off points for connecting further.

The next step is to "awaken" the connector in you, through them. This means opening yourself, possibly further than you have in the past, to meeting the friends, family, and associates of your current "key" friends. Talk about this exercise with them as a starter, and explain that part of your Launchwork is to meet new people you have identified as "connectors." Tell them you are open to invitations to parties, events, fund-raisers, anything, while practicing your connectivity potential. This exercise will show you how willing people are to open up their lives and make connections for you, and also show you how easy it is to be a connector yourself.

Abundant connecting. Operating from a perspective of "abundance" leads to more connecting. Negativity and scarcity get in the way of connecting. Take a look at the following examples and see which category you fall into. If your knee-jerk reaction is negative, don't worry, we've all had thoughts like these. The point is to change your thinking so that connectivity becomes your habit.

A woman gets a new client and calls her friend to share the news. Her friend can respond from a "scarce" point of view or embrace her "connectivity":

1. Scarcity: "She got a new client, which means I have to work even harder to land my own clients because that's one less client in the pool of clients out there."

2. Connectivity: "She got a new client, which means that her success and connection to that new client could mean great connections or ideas for me, and everyone we know."

Here's another example: Two single women go out and meet one very cool single guy. He is attracted to one of them and asks her out to dinner. The other woman can look at this situation from a "scarce" perspective, or a "connected" one:

1. Scarcity: "He asked her out, not me, which means that there's one less guy out there and I'll have to work even harder to find one for myself. I shouldn't go out with her anymore."

2. Connectivity: "He asked her out, which means that her connection with him could lead to connections with his friends, his life, and it also means she's good at connecting. This could also mean that her having a relationship will lead to me having one because I'm good friends with someone who attracts interesting guys. I'm around attraction, which is closer than not being around it."

Now it's your turn. Consider your scarce points of view, written in your launch journal, and then switch them to abundant or "connectivity." If you get stuck, quickly call the most positive person you know. Our successful Ladies Who Launch understand that when they maintain an abundant point of view, choose to be optimistic, and surround themselves with people who think the same way, the more success they will have. Of course they have fears, bad days, or get cranky, but it's their general outlook that produces the results, and the community surrounding a person has an impact on that. Has this exercise brought to mind some of your scarier thoughts? Fears of failure? Perceived incompetencies? If so, write them down and try to transform them to a positive perspective as you go forward in your life. Start to observe how you react and check to see if your connectivity is working at high levels. Here is an example of what a "fear" will look like and what you can do to transform it.

Fear: I want to start a side business without quitting my job but already my husband thinks we don't spend enough time together. How can I justify this additional time commitment, even though it would be exciting for me to launch something?

Fear response: If I can include my husband in some way, then we will be spending time together on one of my dreams. Even if we aren't always together when we are working on it, we will have this in common to discuss and work toward.

Fear: My family accuses me of having Attention Deficit Disorder. They think I don't stick to one thing long enough to see it work out, and think that all my "creative juices" are flowing a little too much. I get ridiculed constantly for starting up some new venture or project, so no one takes my latest ideas seriously.

Fear response: Creative people need to always be creating. One idea leads to the next, which leads to the next. The process is a totally natural one for many women. Part of having tons of ideas is the need to execute some of them at least partially. Try to respond positively by saying that life as an entrepreneur/artist/creative (insert whichever applies) is one that means launching new ideas all the time. If they'd prefer not to hear them, you can offer not to tell them about your latest (this will make them feel like they could be left out, which no one ever wants to be.)

Wingspan: get some! This exercise involves making new connections. During the next week, there will be opportunities either to initiate a conversation with someone or to shy away from one. Do what feels appropriate for you, but see if you can stretch your comfort zone a little bit and talk to someone new at a board meeting, while waiting for your kids after practice, in line at the supermarket, at your husband's office party, or at the gym. One twenty-something young woman bit the bullet and approached a guy in her weight-lifting class. Her only comment to him was something offhand about how hard the workout was, but the conversation led to a hometown in common (Boston), friends from high school from the same year, a mutual friend having a party in their town, and overall a new contact. One minute they were strangers, the next, easy acquaintances. Having random conversations with people is not the point of the exercise, although we don't see anything wrong with that. The idea is to experience a way of living that invites a wider circle of friends, to encourage richness, and to stretch within your own areas. You can retreat from the world at any time (we do on a regular basis!), but try making a new connection every day and see how your world expands in just one week. Make it like taking a daily social vitamin or drinking your usual latte. Everyday practice will yield results, build confidence, and make you (and your life) a more interesting place to inhabit. You can be as subtle or outgoing as you want about it. No one said you had to be Julie, the cruise director from "The Love Boat." It can be as much as asking a girl you know from yoga to grab a coffee afterward, or just chatting a little more than usual with the waiter. Throw out the bait and see what you catch.

Building your team. Building your personal team, the people you rely on to make you stronger, happier, more efficient, and better taken care of, is the next priority. Think about the ultimate team that you would like to have around you. This could include friends, supporters, an assistant, or the guy behind the juice bar. Who do you have on your team who's doing the job, and who is missing? Just like a crew coach would look at her rowing team to see what strengths are solid and what are missing, it's up to you to survey the players and fill in the gaps. If there is an area of your life where you are unsatisfied, this is especially important to resolve. If you are not happy with your body, think about finding a walking partner or a trainer. If you have no idea about how to manage your money, contact an accountant or financial advisor and make an appointment pronto. If you need more girlfriends to see movies with or to go on shopping sprees with, seek them out! You can have a film buddy as easily as a friend who likes to check out new restaurants. If you want to read more, try to create some accountability with someone else and set a goal for one book a month. Look at your life and get a sense of what is fulfilled and what isn't. Maybe you lack a spiritual life and need to think about working with a healer, a psychic, a pastor, or a coach. It could be as simple as taking a pottery class to feel creative again. But it's important to take this time to reflect on what you're not doing enough of, and on who might be a good player to add to the mix.

Through these exercises and expanding your connectivity awareness and skills, you will start to see the pure brilliance of expanding your world in the easiest, most pleasurable way possible. It gives you wings, and a wingspan for your launching.

BOOK RECOMMENDATION

The Tipping Point by Malcom Gladwell. Thanks to Gladwell, *connector* is a common term. Learn more about who connectors are and how you can enhance your connector status, as well as bushels of other sociological and psychographic marketing revelations.

MOVIE RECOMMENDATION

Working Girl. This movie illustrates at least two great points. The first is collaboration. The boss in this movie, Katharine Parker (Sigourney Weaver), is interested only in her own success, recognition, and accolades (hierarchical power), while Tess McGill (Melanie Griffith) wants to create a partnership and contribute with others. She comes up with her big idea by connecting the dots in a perfectly feminine way. The second thing we love is that Tess isn't afraid to radically transform her style to attract future opportunities. She is determined to dress for the role she aspires to, not the one she is in, and she chooses more feminine attire, opting for dresses and stilettos while the other seemingly powerful women around her submit to suits and briefcases.

4

·········

It Is Not All About the Money

I f it's *all* about the money, there's something missing. Women typically do things exclusively for money only when they are financially strapped, but rarely when there are other options. One of the biggest and most interesting characteristics we notice with our Ladies Who Launch is that while they love making money and want to be successful, their motivation for launching is never purely financial. Money can buy freedom and power, allow us to go on nice vacations, to support the charities that mean something to us, to put kids through ballet classes, soccer camps, and college. But women fundamentally have a different perspective about why they launch. It's not that their appetite for money is smaller (we love to spend it and enjoy it as much as anyone), it's simply not the thing that ultimately motivates, inspires, or satisfies women moment to moment. Women are much less enslaved to the idea that our businesses' success is measured by revenue alone. No matter what your relationship and history with money, it is a volatile subject, and can cause serious tension between people. It's one of the most common issues married couples fight about and can be the most conflicted part of a divorce. If you've ever had a friend owe you money for a long period, you know it can be very awkward and throw the friendship out of balance. Yet dealing with money is necessary throughout our entire lives; being clear about how we relate to it and understanding how a good relationship with it serves us is a key ingredient to attracting it.

Our most successful Ladies Who Launch have very good relationships with money. What does that mean? They aren't in denial about the importance of money, and they know what they're worth without being grandiose or overly humble. They see their value and put a price on it. They charge fair prices for their goods, time, energy, services, and products. With products, it's easier to come up with a price that makes sense based on production costs and manufacturing. It can be harder to put a dollar amount on a service. One photographer might charge $500 a day, and another $10,000. The difference in price may be determined by past experience and client list, but self-worth also has an influence. Women, in particular, struggle to put a price tag on what they do, especially if they are working from home or are starting out as a newly freelanced contractor. Many women wrestle with this pricing every day. Are my prices too high? Too low? Am I overcharging or not charging enough? It's easy to feel unsure about what to charge. This is a legitimate concern that can be resolved by seeing what the market value for similar services is, and also with plenty of help (in this chapter) about having a great, even passionate, relationship with money.

Ladies Who Launch rely on their internal compass, rather than their bank balance, when making critical decisions and valuing their products and services. They typically do not sacrifice their brands for financial opportunities that don't match up with their beliefs. They trust that if a seemingly lucrative relationship does not work out, some other, most likely better, partnership will come along in the future. They rely on their instincts to guide them toward the right choices for themselves and their ventures, with confidence and conviction. Some women are naturally programmed in this direction, so it's easier for them to adopt this model, but many of us have been trained out of trusting our gut and are used to getting advice that says, "Take the money at any cost." Our Ladies have made it clear that money is not the end all, be all, but having a healthy relationship with it makes it possible not to be enslaved, tortured, terrified, or seduced by it. A healthy relationship with money means acknowledging what it means to you.

The way we get along with money says a lot about who we are and what we can expect to attract. The truth is that money is the most transformational tool on the planet; we can't do a book on launching without addressing money and our complex relationship with it. Before you can think about accumulating money, paying off your debt, or launching, it helps to look at the role money plays in your life. The questions that follow were designed to help you to take an honest look at yourself and money.

LADIES WHO LAUNCH SURVEY

Are You Stuck in the Traditional Model?

The traditional model dictates that "Money is the bottom line," and money and material goods are the only way to evaluate success.

I feel that I have a good relationship with money; I enjoy thinking
    about it and managing it.   ___Yes ___No

I have a creative outlet that I would explore whether I got paid or not.   ___Yes ___No

I'm thrilled with my current financial situation.   ___Yes ___No

I feel good about my debt.   ___Yes ___No

I have borrowed money in the past to fund a project, start
    a business, or buy something significant such as a house.   ___Yes ___No

I'm great at attracting money.   ___Yes ___No

I think I can be morally upright and spiritually whole
    even if I have a lot of money.   ___Yes ___No

I feel good about charging money for my products
    or services . . . or asking for a raise when it is deserved.   ___Yes ___No

If you said yes to all of the above questions, you have a positive, healthy relationship with money and most likely have a steady or growing bank account. If you said no to even one question, it means you are like many women (and men for that matter) whose relationship with money needs some work! Don't feel bad if your money mojo is on the rocks; it is common for women to have a relationship with money that is fraught with lust one minute and frustration the next. We need money to survive, but it also allows us to shop for clothes or shoes, put our kids through school, and could get us that dream house, maybe with a second one by the beach. This deep desire for money and what it has the power to bring is often matched with some level of anger and angst. Many women feel it's difficult to make enough money and even harder to manage the money they have. Caring about money doesn't mean becoming a slave to it, but this is a heavily charged arena that bears paying attention to. Having a relationship with money means you will care about it; and you'll understand it. To attract money, just like attracting the right job or right partner, you have to "get along" with it. This means stop seeing it as the enemy or blaming it for what is missing. Money is one of those issues in life that gets the brunt of a lot of blame. "If I had more money, I would . . ." or "It takes too much money, so I can't do what it is I want to do . . ." We don't deny that money can stop you from doing certain things, but we like to approach it from the point of view of having a relationship. It's easier to deal with money than you think, you just have to rewire some of those habitual thoughts and break certain patterns to feel a reversal of fortune.

When you were a girl your parents may have encouraged you to be creative in ways that had nothing to do with earning money: did your mother give you her high-heeled shoes and glamorous beads for dress up, tell you to have tea parties with your friends, or did she take you to art classes? As children our imaginations often take us to wild places of creative make-believe. We write poetry, make collages, and keep scrapbooks. Today we see children coming home from school with colorful papers and projects that remind us of how creative we once were. They use glitter, chalk, finger paint, and clay. Their senses are stimulated; they are inspired to create. As a child, you're not painting a picture to sell to a gallery, or weaving a chain of clovers to hawk at the flea market. Your artistic talents are blossoming just for the pure pleasure of creating, and nothing more. What happens later when we enter adulthood? Suddenly the very activities you were encouraged to do became the things your parents told you that you could never make money do-ing. Not only your parents sent you this message, but society at large, their friends, the media, your teachers, and mentors, too. Women are born creators but the tremendous value our society places on money often drowns our instincts while simultaneously devaluing creativity. So we submit to the counterintuitive traditional model by placing our-selves in jobs and on career paths with big revenue potential (at the ex-pense of what we really want to do), which often means following a corporate (or just less interesting) route. We may suffer but at least we know what we'll get in return.

Alternatively, we can attempt to prove to ourselves and society that we can make money doing what we love. In this scenario, we might follow the creative path, using the mind-set that although we'll do what we want (paint, write, act, sew), the price will be our financial security. The traditional model places money and creativity in direct conflict with each other, and sends the message, over and over again, that the more fun it is and the more creative, the harder it will be to make money doing it. With messages like these looming in our heads all the time, it is no wonder we agonize over money, creating the very negative energy that sabotages actually having money. Money flows more freely when we're in the groove, in the flow, activating our skills. People with loads of money may be happy or depressed, but what they are doing right as it relates to money is not disagreeing that money should come their way for whatever reason. They aren't deny-ing it. Many women feel somehow that if they are not suffering and doing something every minute of the day they do not deserve to have money. We have convinced ourselves that money equals sacrifice and that somehow we are not entitled to it unless we suffer to get it!

There is another way. Believe it or not, the quest for money can be fun. Money can be light, easy, and a great motivator for success. Money is one of the most important components to launching, and the better a person's relationship with money, the better the odds of success. Un-derstanding that women approach money and launching in a different way can help you feel more "right" about yourself and your natural tendencies, which will ultimately help you attract more money.

Self-Esteem and Money

Money is a tool, a resource, and in many ways it is an extension of ourselves. Our relationship with it and if and how it comes to us is often a reflection of our self-esteem. This rather startling fact was reflected in the results of our survey.

LADIES WHO LAUNCH SURVEY

Do You Feel Good About Yourself?

	Revenues Greater Than $1 Million:	Revenues $500k to $1 Million:	Revenues $100k to $500k:	Revenues Below $100k:	Corporate Ladies:
Strongly Agree	58.3%	56%	53.9%	48.0%	34.9%
Agree	41.7%	40%	40.4%	45.6%	53.5%
Neutral	0%	4%	5.7%	5.8%	8.8%
Disagree	0%	0%	0%	.6%	2.8%
Strongly Disagree	0%	0%	0%	0%	0%

Do all people with money have higher self-esteem? Maybe. But perhaps the saying "Do what you love and the money will follow" is true. Money in and of itself doesn't necessarily lead to higher self-esteem; in fact many of the corporate women surveyed are making more money than our Ladies Who Launch. Self-esteem can vacillate depending on how they came upon their wealth. Ladies Who Launch report that even though they may not bring in as much money, the self-esteem that comes from doing something that they love and being successful cannot be replaced by it. Launching Ladies make their own choices about jobs and careers, which means they feel better about themselves. A healthy income is a by-product of this internal satisfaction. Fortunately, no matter where you fit in, a better relationship with money is something that you can nourish and develop.

. . .

Portrait of a Lady

Jenny Gering, a fashion stylist for "real women," helps people express their unique style by mining their existing wardrobes to create new combinations and shopping for new items. Jenny joined the New York Incubator after her company had been up and running for one year because she was struggling with how and what to charge for her services. "I was a classic textbook case of a woman undervaluing herself," Jenny said. Feeling insecure about who her clients were and what they could afford, Jenny would practically apologize for charging for her services. In spite of having more than ten years of experience as a stylist for film, TV, commercials, and music video production, including working with well-known celebrities, Jenny continued to feel a complete lack of confidence with respect to charging for her services and became embarrassed each time she revealed her hourly rate. The Incubator ultimately gave her the support system and the tools to overcome her fears and the more confident she became about the value of what she was offering, the more opportunities seemed to come her way, even as she began to raise her prices. Today, Jenny has been hailed by the Wall Street Journal, InStyle, Daily Candy, *and Fox 5 News's "Good Day New York" for her innovative, uniquely customized solutions to the dilemma of creating one's signature style, and charges hundreds of dollars an hour for her services.*

The relationship between money and women is complicated. There is more than a little judgment and hypocrisy when it comes to having money. We live in a culture that flaunts it whenever possible, yet we aren't supposed to acknowledge that we really (really) like it. Somehow this seems at odds with itself. It should be okay to express our affection for the green goddess, money, without feelings of sheepishness. Some of our Ladies feel guilty or ashamed about desiring money. Maybe you have some of those feelings, too.

It's no wonder that fields like fashion, education, and publishing are loaded with women and don't pay a lot in most positions. A woman will more likely make her career decisions based on her lifestyle, passions, and natural talents, or at least have a strong desire to do so, with a dream (if not an effort) to turn those creative hobbies into a day-to-day operation because women view their lives holistically, not in a vacuum, and are often not motivated toward a single goal. We have many goals that need to coexist, and the equation doesn't always include money as the first target.

LADIES WHO LAUNCH SURVEY

What Is the Minimum Amount of Net Income You Would Settle For to Earn from Your Business in Order to Keep Doing It, Whether on the Side or Full Time?

	Featured Ladies:	Launching Ladies:	Launching Gentlemen:
Anything would be fine, I am doing it for fun.	7.1%	7.6%	1.8%
Less than $50,000	14.3%	25.2%	7%
$50,000–$100,000	28.6%	34.7%	24.6%
$100,000–$250,000	14.3%	13.6%	40.4%
$250,000–$500,000	7.1%	3.7%	14.0%
$500,000–$1,000,000	7.1%	2.1%	3.5%
$1,000,000–$5,000,000	0%	.5%	3.5%
More than $5,000,000	3.6%	.9%	1.8%
I'm not stopping until I have an empire like Martha Stewart.	17.9%	11.7%	3.5%

The results from this survey validate our premise that while women would like to make money, they would settle for a much lower payday than men to be fulfilled and, in this case, fulfilled launching their own business. In the Ladies Who Launch community, we see women who are fully content and happy with what they have created. They desire to grow creatively but not necessarily quickly or monetarily in the traditional "high growth" culture. Sometimes they want to put off growth until it makes sense for them personally; a concept that men often find difficult to understand.

. . .

Portrait of a Lady

Clara Rankin Williams started Clarabelle Collections, a high-end jewelry company using a special patented technology for her clasps and semi-precious stones imported from Italy, not knowing how quickly her business would take off. Around the same time, she and her husband decided to start a family and had two children in quick succession. Although she operates Clarabelle Collections from home, Clara wants to wait several years before expanding her business so that she can spend time with her children and focus on her house. However, her business has been very successful and at times she fears getting the word out too soon, or worse, not seizing opportunities that might be coming her way. She believes that moderate growth gives her the chance to spend time with her children and thoroughly think through decisions to perfect her business as she moves forward. To achieve this balance, she has created an alternative work environment: she hires people who work with her at home on the business and who also help with the caretaking of her children.

Just as men are primarily producers and much of their drive is to make more money, take care of their families, and build, women view their lives through a different kaleidoscope, one that doesn't isolate any particular life aspect, and they operate with a desire to satisfy all the elements of their lives in a nonlinear, overlapping fashion. This means that our trademark attorney might also be our best friend; we might be on a conference call while shopping for shoes; we're likely to incorporate yoga into a business conference, bring our laptops to the beach, seek out friends as financiers, or take buying trips to Italy that also include a cooking retreat. Women read lifestyle magazines that give us a taste of everything that interests us: travel, beauty, style, success. Without discounting the *Wall Street Journal, Financial Times,* or *Investors Business Daily,* most women would prefer to read *Lucky, Real Simple,* or *O, The Oprah Magazine,* if given a choice. Sure, there are plenty of women who read financial papers regularly and enjoy it. In general, though, women desire content that speaks to their lives and all the various components of them.

With respect to money this means that women might not always do what it takes to make the most money, especially if it means sacrificing other components of their lives or raising the possibility of leaving those other elements void. When given the chance, women will make decisions based more on freedom, flexibility, and joy than their bank accounts. We are the first to understand that some women do not feel that they have the luxury to think about their freedom, flexibility, and joy; they have to think about taking care of their children and paying the mortgage. But what we are saying is that for women, working for love and passion, with money as icing on the cake, is the ideal.

· · ·

Portrait of a Lady

When Georgia Lee, *director of the highly acclaimed film* Red Doors, *dropped out of Harvard Business School during her first year, she worried about the extent to which this move might damage her relationship with her traditional Chinese parents. Prior to Harvard Business School, Georgia had experienced a successful career at one of the world's top consulting companies and she was living her traditional Chinese parents' dream; she had been making lots of money in a financially secure job. Her trajectory was clear and predictable. But, in contrast to the gray suits and office towers that colored Georgia's everyday life, the film director's chair called to her. During her years as a Harvard undergraduate and then later, living in New York, Georgia discovered she had a passion for filmmaking. While working in consulting, she negotiated time off to take film classes at N.Y.U. and later to apprentice with Martin Scorsese on the film* Gangs of New York. *With a dreamy cinematic experience under her belt, her deepest cravings for film were temporarily sated. The risk-averse parental voices soon loomed in her head and she continued down the traditional path toward Harvard Business School. But Georgia had a personal spreadsheet that mapped and weighed the life and work variables that she believed would make her happy. She went back to it again and again and the results were astounding, even to her. They showed that the best-case scenario of continuing on her expected path of becoming a CEO in a Park Avenue office yielded a life of far less happiness than the worst-case scenario of pursuing the renegade path—being an obscure filmmaker whom no one might notice and with little money to support herself. While the decision to leave Harvard during her first year of business school was agonizing, particularly because it caused a rift with her parents, she could not get the spreadsheet results out of her mind. She felt she had been guided by forces beyond her control, and knew in her heart that she had done the right thing by following her dream. Even when she won the 2005 award for Best Narrative Feature in the New York Narrative category at the Tribeca Film Festival, she felt as if she were living in a fog. Slowly her new reality became her life: she had chosen to live her dream as a filmmaker. Today* Red Doors *has achieved national distribution, she is working on her next feature,* Forbidden City, *and her family is proud and supportive.*

Society's Financial Expectations for Women

We have found another reason that women are less motivated by money—women traditionally haven't been expected to "bring home the bacon." This doesn't mean that there aren't droves of women out there single-handedly putting food on the table for their families, but we believe the lower expectation for women and money has actually given women much more freedom than it's given men to take risks and make less money doing something we love. Society often applauds a successful woman who gives up her career to follow her dream, manages the growth of her business, takes care of her children, or becomes a teacher for less money but more fulfillment. When men make the same decisions, people sometimes judge them, silently or otherwise. Just as it's socially acceptable for women to wear more color in their wardrobes and highlight their hair, men are considered "artsy" or "metrosexual" when they do exactly the same thing. Men get away with more in very urban centers where anything goes (New York, Los Angeles, Miami, London, and so on) but women (generally) are allowed to be more creative in our culture. What's okay for us is more of a "statement" for guys. Some women see this lowered expectation as society looking down on them, but we think it is a great advantage and presents women with a freedom that they should learn to embrace. There's plenty of room to benefit from these differing expectations and freedoms.

. . .

Portrait of a Lady

Kristi Amoroso, called a "wedding goddess" by a client quoted in San Francisco Magazine, left a lucrative family business to create big production weddings and other special events. She strives to marry her creativity with a flexible work schedule so she can be a part-time stay-at-home mom. She consistently tries to work twenty hours a week so that she can spend time with her three small children. Although her business has grown to a point where she could either hire several full-time employees and train them or continue taking selective jobs and doing most of the work herself, she has decided that for the next few years she wants to opt out of managing people, which she admits is probably an even bigger job than simply doing the work herself. She is incredibly passionate about her business and she has no interest in doing anything differently in her business or her life for now, even if it were to mean more financial reward.

Financing Your Business

It is vitally important for women to be educated about all their choices when embarking on a business enterprise, and there is room for women in general to be better educated about finance.

There has been a lot of research lately that implies that women have little access to capital, meaning that they have been excluded from the so-called old boy's network and the millions and billions of dollars that go toward funding male-owned businesses. This lack of access is touted as the reason that while there are close to 11 million women-owned businesses in the United States today, only a fraction have revenues of $1 million or more. According to the Center for Women's Business Research, only 6.6 percent of the U.S. businesses with more than $1 million in annual sales are owned by women. The 2004 report from the Ewing Marion Kauffman Foundation states that less than 5 percent of venture capital investments have historically gone to women. We wonder if it is because women have been excluded from the traditional networks and have less access to capital, or if there are other forces at work. These questions come to mind: first, why are women expanding their businesses at slower rates than men? Second, why is the media and society so quick to assume that this is a problem? And third, if given the choice, would women do things differently? Could it be that the high-growth, quick-exit strategies that are a prerequisite of traditional venture capitalists just don't work for women, causing them to turn away from these opportunities rather than embrace them? Could it be that women want their businesses to grow more slowly, with steady increases and long-term growth, because that's what fits into their lifestyle? Before we explore answers to these questions, let's take a look at how venture capital works.

Venture Capital

Traditionally, if you are not going to self-finance or borrow from a bank, there have been two kinds of investments that businesses have used to get started and take them to the next level: seed or "angel" money and venture capital. Typically seed money is used as start-up funding. It is a small amount invested by individuals or groups of individuals who are also referred to as "angels." These people are usually friends, acquaintances, or people who simply think you've got a damn good idea and want to be part of the action from the get-go.

Venture capital is comprised of larger funds, typically invested using a more formal financing structure and designed to take a promising business to the next level. Venture capitalists usually become interested in a company once it is somewhat established, has proven its ability to produce revenue, operates effectively, and shows a platform for substantial growth. Venture capitalists invest money in exchange for a percentage of shares in the company and are mainly interested in high-growth companies that will ultimately give investors a high return on their money in a relatively short time frame (five years or less) by selling the company or taking it public. You're doing something right if a venture capitalist is checkin' you out! But venture capitalists will require some sort of exit strategy so that they can get their money out. This may not bode well for you if your business is what fulfills you deeply and gives you purpose at your core. You would be giving up a part of yourself!

LADIES WHO LAUNCH SURVEY

What Is Your Ultimate Goal with Your Business?

	Featured Ladies:	Launching Ladies:	Launching Gentlemen:
Sell	35.7%	22.6%	51.7%
Have an IPO (go public)	3.6%	9.2%	0%
Run it until it no longer gives me the financial or emotional benefits, and then wind it down	32.1%	46.7%	34.5%
Other (including leaving to children and franchising)	28.6%	21.5%	13.8%

The conflict is pretty obvious. Venture capitalists want a return on their money (translation, you sell your company and bring in millions for both you and the VCs), and many women don't have a plan to ever sell their company (bad news for VCs)! Many women may plan to run their business until it no longer provides financial or emotional benefits and then wind it down in due time. Women are less likely to sell because women are emotionally attached to their businesses and don't necessarily start them in order to turn them over for a sum. They treat their businesses like their offspring. The very idea of selling their businesses or "getting out" is against their nature. While selling can be a good option for some women, and there are plenty of scenarios where women are interested in selling, conditions have to be optimal. More than the financials have to line up for a woman to say yes to selling.

LADIES WHO LAUNCH SURVEY

Would You Describe Your Business as Fulfilling You Deeply . . .
That Your Business Is Your Passion?

	Featured Ladies:	Launching Ladies:	Launching Gentlemen:
Strongly Agree	78.8%	53.8%	31.6%
Agree	15.1%	36.6%	52.6%
Neutral	6.1%	6.7%	15.8%
Disagree	0%	2.4%	0%
Strongly Disagree	0%	.5%	0%

When a woman pours her passion into something she loves and is very fulfilled doing it, she has to think long and hard about what her next endeavor might be (and if she wants another one right away) before she can even consider selling. For example: imagine you had a home that you loved and adored and had spent months decorating. It has the perfect view, great neighbors, the antique claw-foot tub you always wanted, state-of-the-art appliances, a wraparound porch with an ideal view, and elegant fixtures. All custom-made to your specifications. Imagine someone coming along who really wanted to buy it. It's going to take a whole lot more money to get you to sell than it would if you hated the place or needed to move. For women, businesses are like homes they've spent a lot of time, energy, and love decorating; why sell?

So, how are women starting their businesses if it is not through the traditional models of venture capital? Many women are self-financing, borrowing from friends and family and growing organically. Women instinctively bootstrap when starting a new venture. Bootstrapping is a means of financing a small firm without raising equity from traditional sources or borrowing money from a bank. It is doing as much as possible with as little as possible, kind of like turning a really pretty scarf into a skirt, or making dinner with only what you've got on hand. Bootstrapping relies heavily on the entrepreneur's personal fund and equity. These could include credit cards, second mortgages, personally guaranteed loans, family sources, and customer advances. Bootstrapping reduces the need for expensive external capital and limits downside risk while maintaining upside potential. While bootstrapping positions an entrepreneurial firm to seek outside equity after having proven the viability and potential of the business, the downside is that it may slow down business growth, lead to a loss of opportunity, or even put you at personal financial risk.

· · ·

Portrait of the Ladies

Lindsey Wieber and Gwen Whiting, cofounders of The Laundress, had a great idea for high-end, fragrant fabric-care products but needed to garner the resources to research and launch their idea. To start they threw a party called "Soapsplash"—a for-profit fund-raiser to raise money for the business. They invited their friends of all ages, their families, their parents' friends, ex-boyfriends, *and charged them a fee of $30 at the door and accepted donations. One friend donated the alcohol. Another gave them the party space. Lindsey and Gwen paid for the food. It cost them about $15 per person for food; fortunately people were writing them $300 checks. During the party, they explained their business concept and that the money raised at the event would go toward researching and developing a prototype of the laundry product with professors at Cornell. They walked away with more than $5,000, which became the seed money for the business. Both continued working at their full-time jobs for as long as possible to make enough money to live and to facilitate the transition of launching this venture on the side. Their next step was to get an SBA (Small Business Administration) loan. They started the application process in May 2004 and got approved for $100,000 in October of 2004 based on their jobs and 401ks. The Laundress products are now carried in more than 300 stores, including apparel and home stores, beauty stores, online stores, and Gracious Homes in New York.*

Note to the Broke or in Debt!

Being broke or deeply in debt can be depressing, stifling, and terrifying. However, the desire and need for money can be a great motivator. For some women, the idea of being "in debt" is scary, while others have been in debt as long as they can remember and see it as a fact of life. We cannot operate as your financial advisors, and hope that you have (or will have after reading this chapter) someone you can consult about your overall financial portfolio. What we can do is help you change the way you see your debt, and to gain an understanding of how you may be repelling money. It may sound crazy to say that you could be sending money away (especially because you need it so desperately), but those who attract money have a different relationship with it than those who do not. Money is yet another thing in your life you're having a relationship with. You have one with your parents, your siblings, your friends, with food, with exercise, possibly with some kind of spiritual practice or belief, and you have one with money. Money is an important part of your life; having a healthy relationship with money means being just as comfortable spending it as you are making it. If you think spending it is easy, look at how you spend your money over the course of a week, and decide if it was easy or not; you'll notice that some things were easier than others. The money for the flowers on your desk, a new lip gloss, a card for a sick friend, and a facial was money you probably didn't mind spending. New tires for the car, the dentist, and the dinner you didn't want to go to were probably frustrated spending. Money represents what we can, what we will, and what we really don't want to do. For example, when you get your bills in the mail each month, do you rejoice at looking at all the things you purchased or enjoyed? Most people don't. We say, why not? If you spent the money, unless it was an awful experience, it was probably on something you wanted or needed. It's all about rethinking the expenditure. Isn't the energy bill a sign of your house being warm and cozy? Isn't the cable bill a great reminder of all the episodes of "The Sopranos" and "Entourage" you watched?

We have heard from the Ladies Who Launch that businesses need to spend money to make money. We define and understand investing as putting money, energy, and resources toward yourself and your dream. What better message to your sense of worth that you believe in yourself than by investing in *you!* Part of acknowledging your financial status is realizing that the actions you took to get there were decisions (good or bad) that you made. It can be hard to come to terms with your responsibility for getting into debt or being in an uncomfortable spot. One thing Launching Ladies sometimes do is look at their business expenses and smile because they see evidence of a business in action! No one wants to lose money, but the alternative is to not have anything going out, and as a result, see nothing coming in.

With your back up against a wall financially, it's amazing how survival mechanisms will overcome fears and creativity can kick in. Needing money can inspire you to make the phone call that you were afraid to make, go on TV when you are terrified of the camera, or send in your book proposal when you had doubts about your ability. It also makes for a much better autobiography. The best life stories always involve some type of moment where the person is evicted, bankrupt, or selling their product on a street corner. Even Phil Knight and Bill

Bowerman, the cofounders of Nike, sold shoes out of the backs of cars in the beginning, when no bank would take them on and most people they approached thought they were nuts! Look at the swoosh now.

. . .

Portrait of a Lady

Elaine Gordon launched her company, Elaine's American Maid, out of sheer necessity. Her company is a maid service that cleans more than 140 homes per week and provides work to about eighty mostly low-income women, as well as teaches low-income women how to open their own maid services. Having grown up in New York City on welfare, Elaine started working odd jobs at a very young age to survive due to her mother's illness. Years later when she herself became ill with a collapsed lung and was forced to be in the hospital, Elaine was determined not to be a second-generation welfare mom. Instead of giving up her cleaning business because of illness, she began calling her friends, farming out her jobs, and earning commissions. Elaine's American Maid was born. Elaine is immensely fulfilled through her business, which literally lifts women out of poverty by providing them with viable housecleaning opportunities. She is now planning to expand nationwide; she has been on the Martha Stewart Living Radio show and recently launched a video, How to Clean Your House in 30 Minutes, and Get an Aerobic Workout.

Elaine's story is a great example of someone who launched from necessity. She was forced to think creatively about her livelihood and launching was literally her only option. Elaine is the ultimate example of a woman who embraced her femininity on many levels, overcame any fears she may have had, and took her life and her work to a most amazing place.

Launchwork

Finding your money mojo. Transform your scarce thoughts to abundant ones. Part of creating wealth and also of launching is to stop seeing things from a perspective of disparity. This may feel too philosophical when you're panicked because the rent is due and you have a loan payment peering over your shoulder, but once you get your mind around it, things will shift in a positive direction. Here are some examples.

Scarce thinking: "I can't make an investment in a business when I can barely pay my rent."

Abundant thinking: "Through a small business loan I could start something that would help me never worry about paying rent again."

Scarce thinking: "I can't eat at that restaurant because it's too expensive."

Abundant thinking: "I could eat at any restaurant I choose, but for now it's more fun to find smaller secret places no one has heard of."

Scarce thinking: "I'm cautious with money, which is why I have anything at all in my savings account."

Abundant thinking: "I respect money and spend it freely when I want to, and also have plenty more in my savings account."

Now write down some of your scarce thoughts. When you've come up with ten, turn them around to create abundant ones. This might take a day, so leave the assignment out on your desk so that when you have scarce thoughts, you can write them down. When you're done with the assignment, find someone to explain this process to. Make a phone date, a coffee date, a drink date, anything. Read them your old list first, then read them your new one. This is one part "coming out of the closet" about your scarcity thoughts, and another part driving home the message further so that you can be done with not having money, once and for all.

Educate yourself. Make an appointment with a loan officer at a bank, a financial advisor, a venture capitalist, or a successful business person in your community. You could also take a class or workshop regarding finance or watch Jim Cramer's "Mad Money" on MSNBC. Reach out and get yourself educated so that you can make the best choices and take care of your money. Showing interest in money will allow you to better understand it and make it work for you. It also dissipates fear, which is a major roadblock to having lots and lots of money.

Take actions toward attracting money. These questions are designed to help you improve your relationship with money and take action based on your answers.

If earning and having oodles of money could be accomplished simply by embracing your creative self in its entirety, what would you be doing that you aren't already doing?

Action: Take a step toward doing something on the "abundant thinking" list above this week.

Imagine that every penny you spend is an investment in yourself. What investments are you currently making? What do you need to be making?

Action: Make an investment in yourself this week; buy a book, plan a trip, get a haircut, sign up for a class.

Imagine you have no limitations on the quantity of money you could attract because you would use it for the good that you want to do in the world. How much would that be and what organizations or efforts would you support?

Action: Give something today, even if it's only a dollar.

What if you looked at your other resources (your relationships, your abilities, your sense of humor, your sense of style) as equal to or of more value than money? How rich are you?

Action: Write a thank-you note to one of your resources—a friend or family member who has always supported you, the members of club to which you belong, even your dog who always is there for you (and give her a treat).

By allowing yourself to imagine doing what you would love to do *and* being successful, looking at spending money as an investment in yourself, thinking bigger about yourself and money, considering what you would do to help the world with your millions and billions, and, lastly, looking at your other resources that are worth even more than money, like *you*, you will have empowered yourself and be ready to move forward in your life.

RECOMMENDED BOOKS

Rich Dad, Poor Dad by Robert Kiyosaki and Sharon L. Lechter. This is a quick read that illustrates the difference between working for your money and making your money work for you.

The Secret Door to Success by Florence Scovel Shinn. The author and metaphysician lived and wrote in the early to mid-1900s and often uses religious references, but understand the principles behind her words and you will never think of money or success in the same way again.

RECOMMENDED MOVIE

How to Marry a Millionaire. Marilyn Monroe, Betty Grable, and Lauren Bacall play three dames in New York trying to land a trio of wealthy husbands. Of course, it's never as easy as it might seem, even for the beautiful and talented. This is a great reminder of the fun and adventure money may bring, but also of the qualities money can't ever touch. If these three stunners had spent half as much time building their own lives, interests, or endeavors as they did chasing handsome wallets, they might have become self-made millionairesses!

5

·········

Just Start!

Jumping In Using Your Creativity and Intuition

Is there a little voice inside you that has said, "This person appears to be nice, but there's something that holds me back from getting closer to them?" That voice is your intuition speaking and telling you, for whatever reason, to be careful. Intuition is at the heart and soul of every woman, and is a common characteristic guiding our most successful Ladies Who Launch. Intuition and creativity are fundamental spokes in the wheel of launching, and quite frankly, of living! Some women don't define themselves as creative because they don't feel their core capabilities reflect the talent of an artist. They're not designing buildings, appearing on "Project Runway," or creating like filmmaker Sofia Coppola. A creator, as we define it, is someone who's an originator of ideas, and an innovator who has a broad imagination. Everyone can imagine. Everyone can be creative, whether it's with numbers or paints.

Creativity is the essence of every Launching Lady we have ever interviewed. It's the lifeblood of a woman. A woman's visions, her ideas, her imaginings, are what she relies on to direct her to the next project, idea, house, job, friend, or boyfriend. She has to dream of it and imagine it first, before she goes after it. We are creative beings, literally, designed to create and birth. The source of your creativity is that internal point of view that makes you unique and different, that tells you which direction to take at a crossroads and helps you out of an uncomfortable jam. Some people call it instinct, a sixth sense, or a personal GPS system. Intuition is listening to your voice (it's always speaking, but are you hearing it?) in order to express yourself in the fullest way and create a life you want to live. Learning to listen and then translating your creativity and intuition into something real is often a battle, but it's so much fun. It's one thing to have a creative thought; to actually execute it is the difference between launching to the moon and staying in the Cape Canaveral parking lot.

Creativity itself is an important part of the feminine spectrum. Creativity is innate. It is so crucial for women that without an outlet for creativity, a woman will be frustrated, depressed, and may engage in addictive behaviors such as overeating, endless TV, alcohol, or drugs. The expression of creativity, either through a hobby, the home, family, or career is what leads to a woman's fulfillment. Creativity can and should infiltrate every area of our lives: from meal preparation, shopping, writing, gifting, leadership, decorating, choosing flowers for the table, vacationing, to the activities we do with our children. Creativity has a place at the table, no matter what.

Do you enjoy and celebrate the creative process? Do you use your intuition to make decisions, and more important, do you trust it? Or are you stuck in the traditional model? The traditional model requires a business plan and a single-minded focus. It involves having things figured out before you get started. The emphasis is on being highly productive and profitable.

LADIES WHO LAUNCH SURVEY

I work in an environment that celebrates my creativity.	___Yes ___No
I enjoy working on many different projects at one time.	___Yes ___No
I enjoy the creative process whether I finish the project or not.	___Yes ___No
I do something creative (from the way I dress, to how I write an e-mail, or to the gifts I give my friends) every day.	___Yes ___No
My home is a creative expression of myself.	___Yes ___No
My clothes and accessories reflect a unique expression of myself.	___Yes ___No

I have a good understanding of what ignites my creativity.	___Yes ___No
I have strong intuition.	___Yes ___No
I listen to my intuition.	___Yes ___No
I trust myself to jump in and figure things out as I go along.	___Yes ___No
I like have fun when I experiment with projects, hobbies, or businesses.	___Yes ___No

If you said yes to eight or more of these questions, then you clearly (and wonderfully) have included creativity and intuition in a big way in your life. Not only are you highly intuitive, you listen to yourself and you have a unique and exceptional point of view. If you said no to three or more of the questions, it simply means that there is room for the Ladies Who Launch program to assist and support you with some creative expression in your life, which will only be better for it. Our goal is to unleash your natural creativity and get you to rely on yourself for guidance.

Focus? Hocus-Pocus

"I have too many ideas and I am not sure what I want to do. My boyfriend keeps telling me I need to focus."
—*Lizzie Treister, Ladies Who Launch Incubator member*

Part of the creative process is generating ideas. For women, this sometimes means coming up with multiple ideas simultaneously, often stemming from the same or completely divergent passions.

Most women who launch do so as a way of expressing their creativity. Their projects and or their businesses are an extension of something inside of them or some way of life that they crave. However, many women come to the Ladies Who Launch Incubator with their creativity operating at an all-time low. Maybe they've been working in a corporate job where creativity is neither acknowledged, encouraged, or is downright killed. Perhaps they have their own business but they doubt their creative process because it is not linear or even explainable. They doubt themselves because their creativity and the way many women are creative is not well understood, taught in most schools, or celebrated in our culture. Maybe you were lucky and had a parent who encouraged your creativity, or you went to a school that encouraged and fostered creativity above following the rules and preparing for standardized exams. Most of us were schooled in the traditional model that focused on production. We were graded on linear scales from 0 to 100, A to F. We were taught to finish our homework, work within deadlines, and compete for the win.

One very common declaration we hear from women is "I have too many ideas of things I want to do or businesses I would like to start." Let's get this clear: having too many ideas is not a problem. Unfortunately, many women have grown up learning that certain things—striving for good grades, doing well on the SAT, winning the game—require more of a linear thought process. These skills are all good and important, and naturally we're glad to have the abilities to be able to make things happen. In school most of us didn't have courses in intuition or classes that encouraged being creative with no preconceived end result. Creativity and intuition, these amazing resources of the feminine, are not exercised, teased out, and encouraged. The usual fine arts classes, such as music, theater, and art, are no longer available in all schools due to budget cuts. A woman with many ideas is engaging in her creative process; to reach her ultimate goal she might have to go through several iterations of her idea, sort of like trying on a lot of dresses for a big party until you find one that's just right.

. . .

Portrait of a Lady

Jennifer Coleman, founder of Jennifer Coleman Creative, came to the Ladies Who Launch Incubator program after working as an architect for a large architectural firm for ten years. She had numerous entrepreneurial ideas that crossed into many different industries, ranging from jewelry to hair accessories to urban planning strategies. Instead of being overwhelmed by her many ideas, Jennifer's attitude was to embrace them all at once and create the Jennifer Coleman Creative umbrella that allowed her the flexibility to work on whichever idea was moving or flowing at a given time.

Women are typically nonlinear thinkers and they view their lives holistically. When combined, these characteristics create a powerful, creative, and distinctly feminine force that can lead to all kinds of opportunities, problem-solving, and fulfillment, but only when she learns to embrace this side of herself. Here's an example of how the feminine, nonlinear holistic mind works. Does this sound familiar? Pay attention to the multiple internal voices that literally converse with one another, creating opportunities and unleashing imaginative thinking within her mind:

I was getting a facial at my favorite spa and the quiet time gave me a chance to think. Away from the details and day-to-day operations of my business (fielding phone calls, filling orders, buying merchandise), I had a chance to think strategically about my business.

Internal voice number one: I really need to generate more traffic into my store. I know that once people come into the store, they can't stop buying, but given the remote location and the limited resources I have available to me to advertise, this is really my biggest issue. This is the best facial I have ever had.

Internal voice number two: What if I sent out a promotion to my customers via e-mail that for a limited time only, every person who comes into the store and makes a purchase of twenty dollars or more will receive a facial from this spa at 50 percent off the normal price? It is a win-win for the spa, as I know they are struggling to get more business, too. Why wouldn't they agree?

Internal voice number three: In the quiet time, I am missing my children. It would be so convenient if this spa had a drop-in day care option for moms—they could drop their child off in a small playroom while getting a service. Wouldn't that be great? I think I'll suggest it.

Internal voice number one: On further thought, I should create a small enclosed area in my store where children could play freely and safely while their moms shopped. Literally it would have to be enclosed, almost like a playpen, so moms would not be distracted whatsoever from the merchandise. . . .

Voices intermingled: Speaking of merchandise, I should plan to do a sale soon . . . in fact, maybe I should create an online boutique where all sale items are sold. This would help me get rid of old inventory that is cluttering up the store . . . I could collaborate with other vendors . . . we could design a collaborative Web site for the service. . . . maybe it would turn into some sort of discount mall or something . . . possibilities are endless.

As the above example demonstrates, the feminine mind typically follows a stream of consciousness. Musing on several ideas at once will get you where you want to go, sometimes quickly and sometimes taking longer, but it will get you there. Have you ever had the experience of bringing up a topic with your husband, brother, father, or male friend and he says, "Where did that come from?" For example: you are driving with him in the car, see horses in the field, and point them out. Horses remind you of your best childhood friend who, growing up, was an avid horseback rider. She is now your trademark lawyer. You wonder if you should trademark the domain name you are thinking about buying for a new business idea. It gets you thinking about whether or not the domain name has been purchased. You then wonder how much it would cost to purchase it if someone else owns it. You ask your male companion, "Do you think that domain name is taken?" He's wondering how you got to domain name from seeing horses. The feminine brain experiences thoughts that arrive from many directions, which sometimes collide to form a great idea. To others these ideas may seem unexpected, but to us our thought process makes perfect sense and we are comfortable with how we make connections.

. . .

Portrait of a Lady

W*hen Lizzy Flannagan Carter, founder of Pieces of a Girl, took a cross-country trip with her cousin, she had time to think about her life, her wants and desires. Shortly after returning from her journey, she moved to a brand-new* *city where she knew no one and started a business from her savings rather than going to business school. She knew that she loved to write "love letters" to her friends; she also loved making and creating one-of-a-kind jewelry. When she created a piece of jewelry with its own custom story to go with it for her cousin as a gift, her cousin's response was "This is what you should be doing." Although Lizzie didn't know how she would scale her business or turn her passions for writing and jewelry into a money-making venture, Pieces of a Girl was born. Today, the company continues to grow at a substantial rate and Lizzy has evolved her concept and her revenue streams to include stylish T-shirts with her jewelry-inspired one-of-a-kind story snippets on the back, such as "She's full of courageous surprise and miraculous mischief." She continues to find ways to combine her many passions into her business and she continues to reinvent her business. Best of all her business provides her with the lifestyle and fulfillment that she always craved but never had in her previous jobs.*

Women are often accused of being "unfocused," scattered, or half present. We are usually connecting dots and balancing the many different realms of our lives at once. This isn't to say that men don't also multitask, but women have a bandwidth that seems to stretch for miles when it comes to dealing with the home front, the work front, and the life front. No one thinks it is easy; although many women make it look that way. Connecting the dots, however random it may seem, is how women problem solve and this is how women are creative. What ultimately made Lizzy's business so unique and successful was the combination of her passions: her love of writing and of jewelry-making, which came together in this uniquely formulated way. When we embrace this natural tendency, as Ladies Who Launch do, we can learn to recognize the ability to unite seemingly disparate elements as strengths, not as something that we have to change. We need to do the best we can to harness our creative energy and see it as perfect, just as it is.

Intuition: Your Most Trusted Advisor

Imagine going to the New York Symphony wearing earplugs, or the blasphemy of listening to your iPod while at your child's concert. You would be missing out not only on the recital, but on all the other nuances of the room; the other kids applauding, the parents getting their own children ready, the sound of your beating heart as she takes the stage. When you don't listen to your intuition you are missing out on the wise voice that can point you in the right direction and ignoring information that can lead to your perception of the bigger picture. Your intuition can not only help you find your way, but get you to move!

LADIES WHO LAUNCH SURVEY

I Have Strong Intuition:

	Featured Ladies:	Launching Ladies:	Corporate Ladies:	Launching Gentlemen:	Corporate Gentlemen:
Strongly Agree	83.3%	60.7%	45.3%	56.9%	28.6%
Agree	13.9%	34.6%	41.3%	39.2%	57.1%
Neutral	2.8%	4.3%	12.1%	3.9%	14.3%
Disagree	0%	.4%	1.3%	0%	0%
Strongly Disagree	0%	0%	0%	0%	0%

I Listen to My Intuition:

	Featured Ladies:	Launching Ladies:	Corporate Ladies:	Launching Gentlemen:	Corporate Gentlemen:
Strongly Agree	45.2%	50.9%	36.5%	42.3%	20.7%
Agree	48.4%	39.5%	36.5%	51.9%	51.7%
Neutral	6.4%	9.6%	27.0%	5.8%	27.6%
Disagree	0%	0%	0%	0%	0%
Strongly Disagree	0%	0%	0%	0%	0%

Not only is listening to intuition a key to success for Featured and Launching Ladies, but according to these results, both women and men in corporations are not fully listening to themselves and are downright out of touch with their intuition. We believe everyone has intuition and that women are more blessed than men with that gift. However, over time women are less likely to rely on intuition because it's not valued in the work environment or may even be denigrated at home or among friends. According to the survey results, the Featured Ladies are most in touch with their intuition while other women either know it's there but don't trust it completely, or don't even realize it's living right there inside them, to use at any time.

Without intuition you can't have creativity. It's the difference between doing paint by numbers, which involves being good at following instructions, and letting your creativity flow onto a blank canvas. A paint-by-numbers picture may be beautiful, but it will never be original or valuable. To make something unique and of value, you have to put your personal stamp on it. It's lucky for all of us that just like an artist can improve technique and evolve with experience and practice, you can do the same with your creativity by getting further in sync with your intuition. Launching is really as simple as taking your life experiences, from every textbook you've read, country visited, job held, magazine flipped through, film seen, relationship had, breakup endured, and circumstance experienced, and turning them into some form of expression. We are formed into our unique beings by all of these things; finding some way to express your point of view is launching. It can be as basic as baking cookies with your signature recipe or designing a software program that goes global. What you "create" is a product of who you are at this point in your life, and how you distinguish that is by making it unmistakably you. From your letterhead, to your office furniture, to your e-mail signature, everything is an opportunity to communicate more about who you are.

. . .

Portrait of a Lady

Susie Mendive, founder of SUM Design, moved from California to New York and began working for Stila Cosmetics, helping to help build the whimsical and feminine brand that has become a legend in the cosmetics industry. Along with its easy-to-apply textures and array of colorful shades, Stila became known for its innovative packaging and cartoonist fashionista illustrations, all of which Susie helped to inspire and create. When she first started at Stila, Susie never could have anticipated feeling creatively bored or uninspired. But when Stila was sold to a large cosmetic conglomerate, the small, dynamic company went from entrepreneurial to corporate in a matter of months. Susie began to feel "reactionary" instead of proactive. She felt powerless to make major decisions; she felt that certain opportunities were being ignored. She felt frustrated and found it difficult to move creative ideas forward. She had hit a crossroads. She no longer felt creatively challenged or that she was growing as a designer. At the same time, she began having thoughts about starting her own line of designs that could have broad applications across a range of uses. So was born her idea for SUM, a signature line of home and lifestyle products that are both tasteful and affordable. The underlying distinctive philosophy behind SUM is that if you love a pattern, why not sprinkle it throughout your home to create a consistent theme? Susie says, "There is no reason why you can't apply the same pattern to the pillows on your bed, the glasses on your dining-room table, or the shower curtain in your bathroom." She took her passion for creative design and launched something that was uniquely her own.

Do You Need a Business Plan?

Many women have had it drilled into their heads: must have business plan! They have an inkling of a business idea and everyone is telling them to do a plan. We have evidence to support the idea that a business plan is not always the best first route to go for women, mostly because it stops them before they begin and goes against intuition and "just starting." Jill, a member of the Los Angeles Incubator, wrote seven business plans before giving up and just diving into her jewelry business. When she needs to look for capital, she will have to provide financial information about her company with marketing strategies and retail plans. But many women who have a great idea don't necessarily want to sit down and map it out, step-by-step, as much as their husbands, brothers, fathers, or boyfriends love to tell them to.

What is a business plan? A business plan is a blueprint and communication model for your business. It serves as a device to help you, the owner, set out how you intend to operate your business and also provides a road map to tell others how you expect to get there.

Has the following ever happened to you or anyone you know? A woman has an idea to start something new and some sweet and supportive person inside her school or among her circle of friends, acquaintances, or family says, "You need a plan." If the idea is a business, then the likely statement is, "You need a business plan." So she buys a book on how to do a business plan, searches the Internet for examples, and then sits in front of her computer trying to formulate her idea, to come up with an entire forecast for every possible business scenario. She gets caught up in a perfectionist spiral, thinking she needs to account for every detail, predict every event, positive and negative, and be able to fill in every variable no matter what her experience has been in the industry. Eventually, but not surprisingly, she feels stuck. Instead of moving forward with her brilliant idea she stops out of frustration. What is she going to call it? She doesn't have all the answers yet to the questions posed by the traditional business plan. What is her business model? What is her exit strategy, marketing plan, executive summary, or competitive analysis? The pursuit of her dream gets slowed down, postponed, or worse yet, stopped dead in its tracks.

Why is it that the percentage of women to men in the top business schools is so much lower than in the leading medical and law schools? Women comprise only about 30 percent of the nation's business schools according to a 2004 article in *Bizwomen*. When you consider that women are starting businesses at twice the speed of men and that more than 40 percent of the nation's businesses are owned or partially owned by women, this gender gap in business school feels disproportionate. The truth is, many women are starting businesses without a formal business background, education, or experience, and certainly without a formal business plan. Consider this: Liz Lange, founder of Liz Lange maternity, built her empire without a formal business plan. In fact, she says if she'd had to write one, she probably never would have started! We're not saying that planning is wrong for women. In fact, as we have stressed before, planning is key to designing the life you want. But a traditional, by-the-book business plan per se can often overwhelm us, keep us from moving forward, and act as a fear-intensifier. Below is an example of the creative feminine brain at work on an entrepreneurial idea and how it gets stuck when she tries to think about conforming to the traditional business plan.

Susan is having a leisurely afternoon at the playground with her two children when she is struck with a brilliant idea. What about creating a line of fashion-forward play clothes for moms? These would be clothes she could wear without fear of having them ruined by baby feedings or mud-playing kids— they would be so comfortable and washable that she would be more likely to want to engage in invigorating play indoors and outdoors with her children; at the same time, they would be totally cool, hip, colorful, and versatile. She would feel equally inspired and confident wearing them to run out to the grocery store, to yoga class, or to a casual lunch or playdate with a friend. It would be Juicy Couture meets Adidas, but with lots of options, cuts, and styles. She begins to dream about her idea. She imagines her clothes in Target, selling them online, doing a demonstration on "The Today Show." She envisions layers, hoods, the softest fabrics, flared and flattering pants. She is excited. She is so creatively invigorated that by the time her husband comes home from work, she is like a new person and it is no surprise that she greets him at the door with a summer fruit almond milk smoothie, the colors of which she decides will be the palette for her first set of garments. Over dinner, she dares to tell him of her dream idea but before she can get the second sentence out, he says "You need to put together a business plan. There are no guarantees. You will need financing, investors, and a solid revenue model that takes into account the fact that you will have production costs due before sales come in. Why would you want to put yourself through this anyway—aren't you having fun taking a break now that the kids are in school full days?" That is all she needs to dampen her enthusiasm, Susan is completely demotivated and discouraged. The thought of having to write a full-fledged plan is daunting. She never went to business school; she doesn't know where to begin in terms of projecting revenues and expenses, or putting together a profit-and-loss statement. She is paralyzed, discouraged, afraid. She was about to "just start" but now she is "just stopped." Where will she go from here?

This example is typical of women who come to the Ladies Who Launch Incubator. They have an idea, a dream, or something they want to start, but they are stuck. Most often they are stopped due to the negative voices of others pushing the traditional model for launching something down their throats, or by the voices of society that they have falsely internalized as their own. Considering business plans, especially, can have this unfortunate effect and cause women to feel that they "need" one. If they are not following the traditional model, women immediately assume they're doing it "wrong."

Less than half of all women and men we surveyed actually wrote a business plan to launch their business, and only 34.1 percent of those who did identified themselves as having revenues of more than $1 million. What does this tell us? In the traditional model, planning is key, and, in order to get financing, a business plan is often the required currency. We aren't saying that business plans are wrong or evil; we believe that at certain points in evolving a business, they serve a very important role. A business plan becomes especially necessary when trying to raise money, pitch investors, or borrow from a bank. Actually, the process of thinking through a business from the standpoint of revenues, expenses, and strategic planning is valuable, if you are clear about what it is you want to do. However, often this clarity does not strike until you are one to three years or more into your

WOMEN WHO LAUNCH SURVEY

Did You Write a Business Plan to First Launch Your Business?

	Revenues More Than $1 Million:	Featured Ladies:	Launching Ladies:	Launching Gentlemen:
Yes, I wrote one.	34.1%	46.4%	33.3%	40.4%
No, I plan on writing one in the future.	9.8%	14.3%	24.8%	14.0%
No, I never plan to write one.	24.4%	7.1%	12.0%	29.8%
I have no idea how to write one.	4.9%	3.6%	4.8%	3.5%
I have done an executive summary.	0%	3.6%	7.9%	1.8%
I have run the numbers and have evaluated the company without a formal plan.	26.8%	25%	17.2%	10.5%

venture. Some could spend years on a business plan without ever venturing forth to prove the concept. For those who take the trouble to do one, the calculations are often not at all what they thought they'd be when put into real life. Many women's plans are an evolutionary, creative process to be enjoyed and embraced. Success to them is relative; expected revenue may not be enough to impress a venture capitalist or bank or loan officer, and "personal satisfaction" is not going to win her any serious investors. Creativity brings passion and joy and cannot always be defined in the written form of a business plan, and can definitely not be rushed. Forcing or overly controlling creativity is like trying to make a baby eat when she doesn't want to, telling a tree how many branches to grow, or asking a flower to bloom on demand. Creativity can be enhanced and techniques taught, habits formed and experiences had, but ultimately it requires a supportive environment and time. Creativity doesn't do well under outside pressure, and it takes a certain amount of space and patience, things that we don't have an abundance of in our culture.

Intuition drives creativity; creativity drives action. Our feeling is that action can be a business plan, if that's what you want, but that it doesn't have a very strong relationship to either the intuitive response to launching, or creativity. In fact, it can stop it if it's too early in the launching process. An idea has to get off the ground and get its feet wet, if possible, before "serious" plans are laid. Women like to see what they can create before they set out for world domination!

. . .

Portrait of a Lady

Elizabeth Mateo, founder of Casa Naranja, came to a Ladies Who Launch Incubator with a dream of starting a networking organization for upscale Latina women. As a Latina, she could not find an organization that addressed what she saw was a growing need in the marketplace for camaraderie and connectivity among motivated, trend-setting Latina women. She had been sitting on the idea for years, working on her business plan, feeling stuck, fearful, and unsure of how to move forward. In thinking that she had to write a business plan before she could start, she had inadvertently created a monumental hurdle in her path. When she came to the Ladies Who Launch Incubator we told her to just pick a date and put it on the calendar. Her first event took place two months later and was a smashing success. Today the business has evolved into a definitive online resource for all kinds of lifestyle needs, creating an online Latina community of women and attracting major sponsorships and attention from significant brands, companies, and their Latin employees.

If we had written a business plan when we started Ladies Who Launch, it would have been very unlike the one we would write today. It would have been so radically different that it may have actually prevented us from taking the life-altering paths that we are on now. We could never have foreseen that the Incubator, designed originally as an addition to other courses for women (and to thank our friends for their help), would become one of the core elements of our business, or that our Web site would have evolved into a social networking site where community is an integral element of all the content we provide. Nor could we have predicted that Ladies Who Launch would become a marketing, PR, and distribution channel for the products and services of our members. The reality is that the sacred business plan may have destroyed all possibility of these opportunities: we would have made or not made choices based on whether they made sense in the context of an early plan. We would have followed outside voices, not paid attention to our intuition; we certainly would not be here today writing this book. But now, today, we are ready to write a business plan and will explore several different financing options so that we can grow, but that is only after four years of developing and proving our concept and finally feeling like we have a clear vision of where we are going (at least for today).

When you "just start," as Elizabeth Mateo finally did after joining the Incubator, and follow your intuition, things take off and often materialize in very different ways than you may have imagined. This is what keeps it fresh. There is a more feminine approach to launching, and if you embrace it, we assure you, there is no turning back. You won't want to.

Launching Attributes

In our survey, the shared attributes of our most successful launchers became clear. The great news is that the attributes that the women have in common are qualities that you can develop in yourself. These four attributes—*risk-taking, problem-solving, unstoppable attitude,* and *bravery*—can be used for whatever you decide to launch and move forward in your life.

The message to take away is: "I jumped in, I went for it; I just started and didn't look back." Successful launchers are resourceful and trust that wherever they land, they'll be okay. Featured Lady Stephanie Johnson launched her cosmetic bag empire after leaving a lucrative po-

Risk-Taking

When Launching My Business, I Felt the Following (Select Two):

	Featured Ladies:	Launching Ladies:	Launching Gentlemen:
I jumped into my business without a full-fledged plan but trusted my intuition.	53.6%	50.3%	57.1%
In some ways, I felt like I didn't have a choice but to launch my business. I was so passionate about it; I just had to do it.	46.4%	39.8%	37.5%
Everyone loved my idea and encouraged me to go for it!	25%	37.8%	30.4%
It was scary taking the leap to launch my business.	25%	27.9%	19.6%
People told me that my idea would not work, but I believed in myself.	10.7%	8.1%	10.7%

sition in a Fortune 200 company. Despite crazy looks from friends and family, she never once looked back after taking the leap. She trusted her sense of what was right and wrong for herself. Stephanie doesn't consider herself a "creative," yet she surrounds herself with great inspiration, creative people, and trusts herself 100 percent. When starting a business, you not only reinvent yourself, but reinvent the process and make it your own, sometimes without a lot of other models to look toward for guidance. There is no manual for your unique product and even if there was, you still have to add your own inimitable twist to make it successful. The best way to figure it all out is to do the research, check out the market, see what others are doing, get a thorough and educated sense of the landscape, and jump in. You'll quickly realize if it's something you want to keep working at, or decide that it wasn't the fun or reward you expected it to be. No sweat. There's no shame in trying on hats until you find the right one. For the record, we aren't saying throw all caution to the wind or quit your job without a source of income and hope that it works out. Part of launching is laying the groundwork first, without letting intimidation or doubt take over. Think of it this way, would you move to a new neighborhood without checking out the housing values, crime rate, local coffee shop, schools, nearest cross streets, and local shopping? You absolutely wouldn't. Treat your new endeavors with the same care and depth of thought.

Problem-Solving

Launchers face obstacles on a daily basis, and by doing so gain confidence in their ability to deal with whatever comes down the pike. Sarah Shaw of Simply Sarah had been selling her patented handbag hanger for three years when her downtown L.A. manufacturer told her they would have to double the price in order to continue to produce the product. This threw her margins into a deficit. With a week between what she had

LADIES WHO LAUNCH SURVEY

I Trust Myself to "Figure Things Out" When Given a Problem or Obstacle:

	Featured Ladies:	Launching Ladies:	Corporate Ladies:	Launching Gentlemen:	Corporate Gentlemen:
Strongly Agree	54.8%	57.9%	41.9%	69.3%	44.8%
Agree	38.7%	37%	52.7%	28.8%	48.3%
Neutral	6.5%	3.9%	5.4%	0%	6.9%
Disagree	0%	1.2%	0%	1.9%	0%
Strongly Disagree	0%	0%	0%	0%	0%

available and the new orders that would come in, Sarah was faced with the frightening possibility of having no one to sew her hanger, a time-consuming and potentially expensive proposition. After a mini-meltdown, Sarah called everyone in her manufacturing Rolodex to solve the problem. The answer lay in a new (and far better) cutting service that then introduced her to a sewing company that was able to nearly match the cost of the previous vendor. Sarah reflects back on the problem now as a blessing in disguise and knows that in the face of crisis, there are always answers. As a small business owner, these crises are usually faced alone, which makes them all the more terrifying. But what launchers learn is to rely on their own resourcefulness, good past relationships, and the ability to keep moving forward in the face of fear.

The way to build confidence and trust in yourself is to overcome obstacles and get yourself through a tough patch. One woman compared it to cooking a Thanksgiving turkey for the first time. Once you do it, you gain a sense of accomplishment and pride that you can draw on to pacify future anxieties. When you are out on your own you need to rely on your abilities and ingenuity to get beyond a crisis. In a corporation you will undoubtedly have colleagues and strict guidelines to help overcome a problem. Going solo means relying heavily on intuition (what is my gut telling me about this situation?), creative thinking (how to get over a roadblock), and the team you've built around you. Although you may be a sole proprietor or be "solo" in your mission (with no employees), you still have a network of people to rely on for advice, support, resources, contacts, and help in an emergency. Freelancers and small businesses really have to rely on this network because it acts as an extended family; reciprocity is always the rule, and it also allows you to feel much less alone in your adventure. The truth is, you're never really alone.

Unstoppable Attitude

The other important element to launching is to feel that you are unstoppable when you really, truly want something. Maybe you need a new computer, a ticket for a sold-out show, or to set up a meeting with twenty people around the country at a moment's notice; you need to bring an attitude of invincibility to making what you need happen.

LADIES WHO LAUNCH SURVEY

I Am Unstoppable When I Really Want Something:

	Featured Ladies:	Launching Ladies:	Corporate Ladies:	Launching Gentlemen:	Corporate Gentlemen:
Strongly Agree	64.5%	53.6%	26.7%	44.2%	37.9%
Agree	29.0%	38.1%	56.0%	46.2%	55.2%
Neutral	3.2%	7.9%	17.3%	9.6%	6.9%
Disagree	3.2%	.4%	0%	0%	0%
Strongly Disagree	0%	0%	0%	0%	0%

Every day launchers have to face their fears and not take no for an answer. The more you take a chance, the more you leap, the more often you say yes, do projects that scare the lip gloss off you, do deals bigger than you ever thought possible, or take risks that give you goose bumps, the more you'll experience your creativity and intuition at work.

Being independent means the risks of being in business fall on your shoulders, right? It's your money, your time, your "safety" that you're putting at stake. Is it scary? Yes! There's no denying that part. It also teaches you, in the fastest way possible, how to speak up for yourself and make sure you get what you want. When it's your brand, your product, your service, you will never settle for just okay, as you may have done while working for others. There's more at stake for you personally and professionally. When it's right, you can take credit for it, no questions asked. This is a fantastic, almost drunk feeling of happiness. The responsibility of all of it can be heavy and draining at times, but calling the shots and never waiting to hear from someone three people removed from you about whether a logo is approved or a press release can go out or a product is finalized is thoroughly liberating. Your passion can speak as loudly as you want it to, with no committee or hierarchy to tell you otherwise.

Bravery

Every leap you make, no matter how large or small, will undoubtedly be preceded by fear—fear of criticism, fear of failure, and even fear of success. So whether it's parachuting out of an airplane or speaking to a large group for the first time, there will be an element of fear involved with anything worth doing. Launchers are risk takers, but the good news is that this bravery is a quality you can develop. You don't have to be born with it. Once you've overcome one fear you will gain the confidence to take on more and more challenges and have the confidence that you will land on your feet.

LADIES WHO LAUNCH SURVEY

I Am the Type to Take a Leap, No Matter How Much Fear:

	Featured Ladies:	Launching Ladies:	Corporate Ladies:	Launching Gentlemen:	Corporate Gentlemen:
Strongly Agree	38.7%	30.3%	12.5%	28.8%	13.8%
Agree	35.5%	41.3%	27.5%	44.2%	41.4%
Neutral	6.5%	17.3%	26.2%	21.2%	41.4%
Disagree	19.3%	10.4%	27.5%	3.9%	3.4%
Strongly Disagree	0%	.7%	6.3%	1.9%	0%

Sooner or later you'll need to take a leap, but not everyone is capable of going full throttle from the beginning. You can be a launcher and take things step-by-step, but think of each step as a leap (it could be as simple as making a phone call), and you will build your confidence to take on a larger challenge. It's okay to be more cautious and not put all your money on the line, all your resources in one basket. Go ahead and deeply research the people who do business with you; you will get to where you want to be by taking measured healthy risks.

Launchwork

The purpose behind this homework is to give you the tools and the support system to achieve and live in what we call the "heightened state of creativity," which means having an awareness of when you are operating creatively or when you are simply reacting to the outside forces around you. When you act creatively, you are consciously problem-solving or linking ideas or concepts that might otherwise seem not to fit, or that others may think a complete mismatch. There is a way to organize your day around having more of this quality creative time, but it means that the more robotic day-to-day tasks like reconciling the credit card statement or filing documents happen in an hour dedicated to doing just those things (instead of dribbling them throughout the day). When that hour (or three on some days) is up, your mind has permission to think the bigger thoughts and possibly have great epiphanies. This is where book ideas come from, new works of art, or a relationship breakthrough. It's about spending less time (or at least separated time) on the "business" of living and more time on living creatively. Once you know how to lay the foundations for the heightened state of creativity, you will want to strive to be in it for as many hours a day as possible, for as much of your life as possible. You will find ways and set up systems so that you can exist in this state with little interruption. When you exist in the heightened state of creativity, you begin to notice and take responsibility for the amazing things that happen in your life. You will bring subconscious thought to consciousness, and live in a true fusion of life and work. Here's how it starts:

Become your own administrative assistant. Look at your day and the tasks that need to be accomplished. Typically, a day could look like this: go to the gym, clean the kitchen, return phone calls from yesterday, research new products for a project, conduct regular administrative communications via phone and e-mail, write a summary of your company for your press kit, take the dog to the vet, and buy groceries. So if this is a general snapshot of your day, you'll want to see if you can aggregate what needs your administrative focus and build that into either the first two hours of your day, the last two, the afternoon, or whatever works for you. Planning and taking care of these administrative tasks allows room and time for creativity. Many people find that they are at their most creative in the early morning, so these are the hours they choose to write, meditate, sew, draw, design, or imagine. In the case of this list, the administrative focus is on e-mails and returning phone calls. The rest are tasks that don't require full-bodied concentration to carry out, which leaves room for the mind to do several things at once. Decide when you want to do your administrative work and stick to it. Yes, you'll get e-mails all day long, perhaps, but if you're interested in being in this heightened state of creativity, it's important for you to dedicate time that is specifically focused on getting bills paid and e-mails and phone calls returned before you go on with your day and let your mind roam a little more. Not every day is going to be like this! But allow yourself at least one day during the week where administrative work isn't the entirety of your afternoon. It might only be possible on a weekend.

Create a "loose list." More than a traditional to-do list, a "loose list" is a series of ideas or actions that can get you moving in the direction of your goals. Each step doesn't follow the preceding step necessarily. They do not have to be done in a specific format or within a certain time frame, and are not set in stone. A loose list is meant to inspire, not shackle you to a lockstep list of items to tick off as you complete them. Using the example of Susan and her fashionable play clothes idea outlined earlier in this chapter, compare a masculine business plan-oriented to-do list with a feminine action-step-oriented "loose list." Remember, your list does not have to be about starting a business, but can be about what you are dreaming of.

Traditional To-Do List (Business):

  Cold-call bank and ask to speak with someone about business loans.

  Conduct break-even analysis; determine whether idea is financially viable or not.

  Draft marketing section of business plan.

Make five-year forecast.

Create cost comparison depending on national economic factors.

Feminine Loose List (Business):

Call a friend in fashion, run idea by her, ask for list of cool
stores in garment district for fabric buying.

Wear the dress to a party and see what everyone says.

Start a fashion biography book club.

Go to a local fashion show and see how one is done, start to
finish.

Watch the movie *Prêt-à-Porter*.

Create a mood board; tear sheets from magazines that inspire you.

Now create your own "loose list." If your list is coming out looking
more traditional, see if you can add some sprinkle, some feminine
dust. Look at each item and ask yourself, what would be the most fun
way to accomplish that? Sometimes, however, there won't be a fun way
to go about applying for a grant or researching.

Embrace risk. Trigger your creativity and enhance your "launcher
talent" by doing at least one risky thing and/or do something new every
week. Try a new restaurant, a new coffee, buy a new CD, or take a new
route to work. Put yourself in new situations, such as hanging out with
a new group of people, trying an improvisation class, or singing. Sell
your wares at a trunk show. Creativity thrives on expansion and curiosity, and creating new environments for inspiration and new vehicles
for delivering it. Look around your life and see what could use some
juice. If you are the person that never talks to your neighbor, give it a
try. If you've wanted to post a profile for online dating but have been
too timid, now is the time. Each week do something that fits into each
of the categories of a "creative and intuitive launcher," and watch how
this expands your mind, increases your belief in yourself, and turns
your life into a constant freeway of forward movement.

Following are some exercises. If you do exercises one through five, we promise you will be on your way to developing the attributes of a launcher. As the name of the chapter states, just start.

1. Jump into something unfamiliar. Take the leap. Say yes to an invitation you'd normally pass on.

2. Be unstoppable. Has someone said no to something that you really want? Go for it again. Ask a guy on a date, go to a different bank for a loan, or insist that the store order your favorite nondairy, sugar-free, gluten-free, no transfats dessert. And do it all with the biggest smile you've ever had.

3. Do something that scares you each week, and if you are really going for it, each day. Strike up a conversation at the dog park, give a toast at a wedding, reveal your feelings to someone special, see if you can run an extra mile, say "no" to someone who is used to hearing "yes."

4. Identify an obstacle that is in your way and come up with creative solutions for getting around it, over it, or through it. For example, when you find yourself facing a problem at work, in traffic, with your husband, girlfriend, or boyfriend, before reacting check out all your options. There is usually a way around the problem, and launchers see opportunity where others find frustration. See if you can't find another road, and then explore why this other path might be even better than taking the usual approach.

5. Incorporate at least one creative activity into your life every day. Here are some ideas:

- Experiment with cooking by taking a recipe and changing one element of it, or combine two ingredients to create an unexpected dish.
- If you have children, instead of reading from a book during story time, make up your own story to tell your child. Create your own characters, plots, and circumstances. Describe places

and clothes in imaginative detail. This exercise is addictive and will become the most popular request from your little ones.

- Buy art supplies and steal a moment to create your own art-work. Experiment with colorful chalks, finger paints, pencils and crayons, or any other materials you can think of (glitter, tissue paper, feathers, or fabric). You may find this activity not only creatively inspiring, but also mentally soothing—a stress buster!
- Spend a day working from bed. Brew your tea, get your lap-top, turn on music, open the windows, and burrow into the covers. Vera Wang has said she does much of her work from bed, and she's a major creator!

These exercises will help bolster your confidence and help you to realize that you, too, are unstoppable. You are brave, resourceful, and can overcome obstacles. Believe it.

RECOMMENDED BOOKS

Kaballah and the Power of Dreaming by Catherine Shainberg. Catherine is one of our most insightful, thought-provoking, wise-beyond-life-on-earth teachers. This book helps you release some of your creative blocks and discover your intuition by teaching you how to understand your dreams while you are sleeping, and also to dream while awake.

E-Myth Mastery by Michael Gerber. A great read that walks the reader through a powerful process of examining the extent to which she spends time doing tasks versus managing people and being creative in her business; it artfully illuminates how to work *on* our businesses instead of *in* them.

Ask and It Is Given by Esther and Jerry Hicks. This read might strike you as "out there" at first, but keep turning the pages. This is one book with guaranteed "Aha!" Again, the laws of attraction are extracted to arrive at stunning and amazingly effective results. Not getting what you want out of life? You will now. Trust us.

RECOMMENDED MOVIES

What the Bleep Do We Know? This thoroughly life-changing documentary will expand your mind and change your way of looking at your thoughts, the information you process, your energy centers, and the fascinating mysteries and revelations behind quantum physics.

The Secret. Watch, learn, change your life in less than two hours. *The Secret* reveals the true laws of attraction and gives insight into bringing what you want toward you. It's not about hard work; it's about something altogether different, and so much more fun.

Part II

· · · · · · · · · ·

The Ladies Who Launch Incubator Program

A Four-Step Process

6
....

Preparation: Fill Up First

Imagine staying up all night working, getting no sleep, and then host-ing a party the next day where you have to cook, clean, socialize, and hostess. Without rest, without fuel, without TLC, you cannot suffi-ciently keep the machine working for very long. It may sound trite, but this advice is of key importance because, as many times as we've heard it, few of us are as disciplined about taking care of ourselves as we could be. Before you can think about launching you have to be well prepared mentally and physically. If you're not doing a stellar job of keeping your sanity as well as keeping up healthy habits, you won't have the extra reserves you need to call upon to launch as high or as far as you can go. We frequently talk to women who are burned-out, stressed-out, and time-starved. They are doing so much for their jobs, their families, and their friends, but so little for themselves. They usually can't imagine how to fit in some "me" time.

We all know that it's important to take care of ourselves, so why is it so difficult? We think it's because we live in a very reward-oriented society. You get a good grade and your parents take you to get ice cream, you agree to vacuum the den and you get five dollars. As you get older, you create your own rewards, which usually punctuate a harrowing task: work an eighty-hour week and you treat yourself to a massage; go to the gym every day for two weeks and then indulge in birthday cake. It's great to reward yourself, but the problem is that women today are overworked perfectionists, who are often taking care of so many people that rewards just don't make it onto the to-do list. When they do get around to a reward it is often a little too late, after burnout has set in and the pleasure is diminished. What if we looked at taking care of ourselves as a creative endeavor, or a productivity strategy?

When you have a head cold you can't think straight, you can't focus, and should probably forget about having a creative thought or idea. Less obvious creativity zappers are a neck so tense it hurts to have it rubbed, or an unhealthy relationship with coffee and vending-machine snacks. A ten-minute massage before the pain gets unbearable is taking care of yourself. Five extra minutes in the morning to make a healthy lunch is taking care of yourself. Drinking water instead of coffee is taking care of yourself. Maybe you still haven't painted your bedroom although you think about it each morning and night. It bothers you, but months go by and for one reason or another, you don't take action. Every time you consciously reject going forward with something, or deny what you know you should be giving yourself, it takes up space in an otherwise creative mind. We call these creativity-suckers, but they're life- and joy-suckers, too.

There isn't a quick answer to how to take care of your well-being. It is a practice; meaning, it's something you "practice" every day. Yoga is a practice, prayer is a practice, communication is a practice, and so should pleasure be! We see it as a discipline, too, and you need to create a plan that is as individual as you are and consider it part of your daily routine. Taking time for yourself sends a message that you are important and valuable. You probably take great care of the things that you love. Sadly, some of us take better care of our cars than we do of our bodies and minds.

A fair warning: it's not easy. You may feel selfish, overwhelmed, or angry with us for suggesting that you stop doing something else and start taking care of yourself. You may feel that taking time to be nice to yourself only gets in the way of getting other stuff done. However, if you take the time and do it with diligence, you'll start to see results in parts of your life where you least expected it. It's just like when you start working out at the gym and gradually start to feel better. Toned abs and leaner thighs shine through, and suddenly you want to do more, work harder, and see how good you can look and feel. There is deep wisdom in the standard airline preflight announcement that we all know by heart: "Please adjust your own oxygen mask before assisting others." When you can breathe easily, others will get the benefit of your strength. That includes husbands, children, friends, coworkers, clients, siblings, and parents. Everyone is better when you take care of number one, and everyone gets more of you when you have more to give.

. . .

Incubator Moment

Tonia Misvaer has a very successful creative services company called 3SL Creative that specializes in design, branding, print production, and paper products. When she came to the Ladies Who Launch Incubator, she was burned-out and had lost her passion for her business. One of the exercises in the Incubator is to do something nice for yourself, every day. Like a dutiful student, she began her homework immediately. Initially, her employees were confused over Tonia's noontime disappearances. She explained the homework to them and revealed that she was leaving the office to get some exercise. Tonia's employees caught on quickly. They began to understand that part of Tonia's sanity and energy was contingent on doing something good for her body. Soon they were asking themselves what it would take to make their own lives more inspiring? Leaving for massages in the middle of the day and going out for lunch became normal practices.

Once Tonia realized that previously she had thought of working out as something that she "had to do," and had not thought of it as filling up, her whole perspective changed. She realized that eating well, taking time to get manicures, and buying flowers for herself were all things that she was either doing rarely or taking for granted. After doing the exercise for one week, her passion came back with gusto. Thanks to Tonia's commitment to her own pleasure, a new and vigorous energy has permeated the office. Believe it or not, business is pouring through the door. It's hard to explain exactly why energy shifts toward pleasurable directions *inspire more business. Our perspective is that people are simply more interested in those who treat themselves with respect. You want to be near and do business with people who enjoy their lives.*

What is your source of rocket fuel? Or maybe we should say, what makes you fly? Is it yoga or kickboxing, avocado or chocolate? Do you like sailing, reading, or gardening? When was the last time you got a manicure, had your hair cut, or went to the doctor, dentist, or dermatologist to make sure you are healthy? Here are a few things to help you design your unique plan to fill you up, recharge your batteries, and improve your outlook. They say it takes twenty-one days to create a habit, and our goal is to make a habit of taking care of *you*.

Launchwork

The recharge-athon. List at least one hundred things that make you giddy, punchy, and almost drunk with pleasure. What do you do that makes you more creative? What are your indulgences? What makes you smile? What gives you energy? Do one hundred things seem like a lot? Good . . . this is a research project that you can continue for a lifetime. This list should constantly get updated and added to, and should be close enough by that if you flip through a magazine and see an adventurous vacation you want to pursue, you can add it to the list. Some of ours include:

Yoga first thing in the morning
Taking a bath at midnight with candles
Lighting incense for no reason
Writing fiction whether anyone reads it or not
Watching movies . . . foreign, classic, corny, and romantic
Sample sales
Icebox cake
Dressing up for the opera or symphony
A latte with chocolate sprinkles
Sixteen-ply cashmere

Reading before bed
Picnics
Playing cards with friends
Discovering a hole-in-the-wall restaurant
Sushi and sake
Clean laundry
Garage sales and flea markets
Reading the Sunday paper in bed
Strolling hand-in-hand with a significant other with no partic-
    ular destination
Farmer's markets
Crossword puzzles
Hiking with dogs

Doing nice things for yourself requires some self-discipline; it doesn't always come naturally and is one of the greatest challenges for many women in the Ladies Who Launch Incubators. Practicing this discipline can make you feel overly indulgent and radically different from what you're used to. Before you can think of one thing for yourself, you'll think of twenty-five other things that need to be done, and more than half of those will be for other people. The good news is, everyone in your life will prosper from your dates with yourself because when you have a full tank of gas, you will have more to give everyone around you.

Once you get started, it becomes easier to carve out time. Women tell us that once they started a weekly bath ritual, their husbands were happy to take the kids because their wives were so relaxed and happy after. Weekly flowers on the table inspired one Ladies Who Launch Incubator member to start doing professional flower arranging. Karla Lightfoot, one of the Incubator leaders in New York, began doing yoga as a stress reliever while attending journalism school and decided to take a teacher training class. She is now a yoga instructor. You never know where these actions will take you. Our results-oriented society may frown on taking time out from the to-do list, but who says these activities are not result oriented? It all depends on your perspective.

Here are some guidelines to support your own custom-designed "well-being program."

- Find a fill-up buddy. Choose one friend (preferably one who is also reading this book) who can check in with you once a week. You do the same for her—and don't be easy! Your role is to make sure she actually puts something nice for herself in her calendar, or that she didn't eat breakfast standing over the sink, or that she made time to work out during the week. Her job is to make sure that you're not the only one walking the dog, that you got to watch your favorite TV show, that you got a pedicure, or called an old friend for an overdue chat. Get it? Stuff that makes you happy should be on the menu, every day.
- Make this the priority in your day. Write it in your calendar or Palm Pilot. Set an alarm. Make sure that this is the very most important part of your day.
- Schedule appointments with others. If you find that you have trouble doing nice things for yourself then make dates that you can't cancel. For example, hire a trainer, make a standing appointment for a weekly manicure, and start a book club so you make sure that you spend time reading.

Now that you have set your wheels in motion and you are filling up your tank, keep moving forward. Now is a good time to make some tea, grab a cozy comforter, and start your list of all the things you love to do. But start this list and keep adding to it. Don't be surprised if you find you haven't done a lot of these things in far too long!

RECOMMENDED BOOKS

2001 Things to Do Before You Die by Dane Sherwood. In case you were having trouble thinking about where to go, what adventure to have, or in what part of the world you might want to live someday, this book will kick you in the tush and probably inspire a ticket purchase!

The Modern Girl's Guide to Life or *The Modern Girl's Guide to Motherhood* by Jane Buckingham. These page-turners offer wisdom that feels as if it is straight from the source of all femininity. Learn everything you need to know about etiquette, hygiene, or how to hem a pair of pants. There is ample coverage on doing nice things for yourself. Similar rules apply for motherhood.

RECOMMENDED MOVIE

In Her Shoes. Watch how these two sisters (played by Cameron Diaz and Toni Collette) transform themselves from desperate and lonely to recharged and happy. One leaves a high-stress legal position while her sister abandons a nomadic, lazy existence in favor of a true passion.

7

. . . .

3, 2, 1, Launch

Now, it's time to incubate! This is one of the most exciting, exhilarating fireworks moments we've ever experienced. When women first come to our Incubators, they don't know exactly what to expect. They're optimistic, curious, and looking for something, but are not always sure "what." After the first session of the four-week workshop, most members can't sleep they're so excited. What is it about putting a group of like-minded women together in a room, united in their interest in launching? This recipe sets fire to creativity and energy, and once the ball starts rolling, it can't be stopped. The energy inside the Incubator is contagious, time after time, and gives everyone in the room the safest, most long-lasting high they never expected. Now, it's time to take you through the same successful process that thousands of women in cities nationwide have gone through to launch their plans in the Ladies Who Launch Incubator program.

Our Incubators are like a breath of fresh air, and a source of unending enthusiasm. Think of an investment club where the investment is your life, or a book club where *you* are the book of the month. The Incubator normally takes four weeks, one night a week. We will be taking you through the process throughout the rest of this book, step-by-step. This process will help you place your attention on your desires and dreams, expand your vision, and get you moving forward. This focus could be anything from relationships to career expansion to taking a business to the next level to travel adventures to something as simple as broadening your idea of what you can do with your life. It can be anything you want to grow. The exercises are designed to help expand and further visualize whatever you put in, by focusing energy on your concept (even if it's the idea of finding a concept). Investing time, energy, enthusiasm, and vision for yourself and those around you will create your own nurturing environment (or Incubator) to expand your project. You can enlist a group of friends to read this book with you, and follow these chapters together, or you can carry on by yourself. You may want to bring in others in the future to continue growth of an ongoing project or to start something new. We find that the best results are done in groups of three or more. Our Incubators are made up of up to twelve women, a number we feel represents the ideal level of contribution that can be achieved by each member. The more people you include in the process, the better. Join a Ladies Who Launch Incubator group and you will experience results even more rapidly. No matter what, doing this with diligence (the fun kind) will lead to movement that will expand and create momentum behind whatever it is that you articulate. Sometimes you have a blank slate coming into the Incubator. This is fine, maybe even better. But this means that it's even more important for you to create a small Incubator of your own, or join an existing one. (Go to www .ladieswholaunch.com to find out if there is an Incubator near you.)

Four Steps to Launch

There are four destinations, or steps, in the launching process. These basic steps have been behind the creation, development, and success of just about every endeavor you can imagine.

1. Imagine it
2. Speak it
3. Do it
4. Celebrate it

This progression often happens organically, but we have identified and arranged the process into deliberate steps that have delivered results to hundreds of Incubator groups around the country, and the world. The process may seem simple, and in a way it is, but if you follow the steps in this book you will start to see significant movement in your project or in your life.

When people ask you what you're doing, tell them that you are incubating and growing an idea using the feminine process. Of course, you can take advantage of more traditional tools that you might need. If you need a business plan to raise money, if you need to form a corporation or put together a PowerPoint presentation, fine. We won't specifically address these tools in our exercises. Hard business tools are important, but we feel that the Ladies Who Launch process is the most intuitive, imaginative, and feminine way to go to new places. Some will be starting a business, while others will be taking an existing business to new heights, creating a social life, or exploring a creative endeavor. Our culture tends to focus on the bottom line and productivity, which doesn't usually allow for the luxury of hanging out with your projects, dreams, and what ifs and letting them evolve in a very feminine and natural way.

The Traditional Process of Embarking

Write the business plan.
Crunch the numbers.
Pitch the idea to potential investors.
Work really hard to make it happen, and when you make your first million gather together your employees for a cake and some champagne in paper cups.

The Feminine Process of Embarking

Take your passion and imagine making it come true in the best way possible, or better yet, making a living doing what you love, or taking something you are already doing in new and profitable directions.
Test the concept with friends by talking about it and getting

their feedback and ideas, honing in on your strategy and point of view.

Start doing it, dipping your toe in, taking some actions, feeling it out.

Have a big ole party to celebrate your first dollar, hundred dollars, or one million (okay, and buy some shoes).

Which sounds like more fun?

The following tips will help you get in the flow and release your creativity as you do the exercises and should be kept in mind throughout the book. Some people even put these on a bulletin board as a reminder throughout the process. Consider these your mantras!

1. Have fun. You'd be surprised at how caught up we can get in the seriousness of our projects. Fun is a creativity releaser. The less serious and the more fun that you can make the process, the more your creativity will flow, the more attractive you will become (people love to be around those who are in motion and having fun along the way. While stress and angst aren't attractive, excitement and curiosity about your potential are very hot!). As soon as you throw on the fun switch, everything comes a little bit more easily.

2. Be a yes. Being a yes means you embrace what is coming your way. We don't mean that you should accept calls from telemarketers or take uncalculated risks, we mean be open to what the universe and those around you are offering. The more open and flexible you are about moving in new directions, taking feedback, and receiving input from multiple sources, the faster you will move toward your dreams. Some brilliant person said, "Say yes to life and life will say yes to you." Yes can be scary and will undoubtedly take you out of your comfort zone but yes opens doors and possibilities.

3. Pay attention to movement. Throughout the process of doing these exercises, we can guarantee that things will move in your life, but we can't guarantee *what* exactly. Sometimes, other things, aside from movement toward your primary desire, happen first. You may

find yourself organizing your home, clearing out your office, meeting a man, or taking an exotic trip. A woman in an Incubator was trying to build her jewelry business, but instead found herself with an even more important piece of jewelry on her finger; she got engaged, got married shortly after, and nine months later had a baby! She eventually circled back to her entrepreneurial endeavor, but focused on her new partnership first. We also had an actress who had mentally checked out of [show]business and wanted to transition into interior design. Ironically, when she started the Incubator, she was suddenly at the receiving end of some interesting acting opportunities. You will get where you are supposed to be, but it can only happen when you are out and engaged in life (being a yes). Sometimes, there are other areas that may take priority over your project or life may take you in new, exciting directions that you couldn't imagine. Finding yourself going in another direction is not a sign that your project isn't moving forward, it just signals that your project will probably excel at another time. The idea is to let go and flow.

4. Include others. There are going to be some extra-credit assignments that involve bringing other people into the loop for your project. Opening to others is a little daunting for some, and you may think that your special endeavor is best left to the quiet interiors of your mind, as your own special mystery. We have done this over and over, and worked with women who practically refused to let their friends and colleagues in on their creation. Ultimately they saw the value of sharing their ideas with their community. The more people you bring in, the more people will be involved in moving your project forward. Ask anyone who's launched a business and she'll undoubtedly tell you that great contacts and ideas came from unexpected places; her friend from high school helped her find her manufacturer, her manicurist recommended a seamstress, and her professor hooked her up with an intern.

Before moving forward it's important to identify your wishes and dreams so that we can take a long and deliberate stride toward making them happen.

. . .

Incubator Moment

Gerry Baum scarcely recognized photography as a viable career path. At best, it was an enjoyable but secondary hobby that was briefly mentioned at the start of the Incubator. Her primary project, by the end of class, had completely evaporated, while photography had replaced it. She was surprised at her transformation from administrator to artist in less than four weeks. This is what getting into the launching mind-set can do. Gerry is a capable, creative woman who was doing work she liked but didn't love. Persuaded by her Incubator leader to consider a secondary project, Gerry was seized by her creative instincts, and stepped into doing what she really wanted to do all along.

Think about what you want to launch. Is there a grand idea floating around in your mind? A screenplay? A jewelry-making business? A relationship? A weight loss? Maybe you know you want to do *something* but need some help pinpointing exactly what. Have no fear. The dozens of exercises, starting with this one and including the others throughout this book, are designed to help you define, expand, speak, celebrate, and most important, move forward with what we will call "your project." If you don't have a specific idea, don't worry, you will name your project soon. There's no hurry.

Which Direction?

Determining which direction to go in, according to our most success-ful launchers, means following your passion, and launching in the direction where you detect the most heat.

For our Featured Ladies, listening (intuition) to what fulfills you deeply (creativity) is the key to the kingdom of happiness, that elusive place that we all strive to find. This is the definitive direction to go in, and for the rest of this chapter, the exercises are designed to help clarify your own passions and set you up to get there.

LADIES WHO LAUNCH SURVEY

Would You Describe Your Business as Fulfilling You Deeply . . .
That Your Business Is Your Passion?

	Featured Ladies:	Launching Ladies:	Launching Gentlemen:
Strongly Agree	78.6%	54.0%	33.3%
Agree	14.3%	35.8%	54.9%
Neutral	7.1%	7.1%	11.8%
Disagree	0%	2.6%	0%
Strongly Disagree	0%	.5%	0%

Dream Wish List

This list is guaranteed to spark something in your quest to find the "right" direction. The idea behind the dream wish list is that if you want it, write it down. Feel free to stretch beyond material items. In addition to a brand-new wardrobe from Saks, perhaps you also wish for better health, more time with your husband, or an exotic trip to Bali. This will be an ongoing list of everything big and small that you want; create a special section in your launching journal. Desire is what makes the world go around; without desires, we are a bit like empty, boring shells of people. Some people think that to have desires means that they have to be able to afford and do everything on their list. Try not to think of the how right now, just think of the what. Have you ever met anyone who didn't have any aspirations or dreams and acted as though there was nothing they could want, either because they've achieved it all or because they're despondent and uninspired? You probably discovered that there isn't much to talk to them about. One of the women in the Ladies Who Launch Incubator dreams about traveling to forty countries before she turns forty, another dreams of launching a publishing company for Native Americans, and another wants to leave her corporate job to embark on a film career. Wouldn't each of them be interesting to sit next to at a dinner party?

The key to this exercise is to let everything out and have fun doing it. See the world as a buffet where you get to make your own plate, with no caloric or health-related consequences. Again, don't bother trying to figure out how you will accomplish these dreams; in fact, strive to make them much bigger than you can imagine them happening on your own. This list is about declaring your dreams, coming out of the closet on yourself. Most important is to remember that nothing is too bold, too much, or too greedy. Smile, have fun, and enjoy your dreams like you would your favorite meal.

Wouldn't it be wonderful if . . .

I could go horseback riding like when I was fifteen.
I could land ten consistent clients.
I had a new journal to write in.
I could make time to write in a journal!
I could visit my sister more often.
I could have my house cleaned professionally once a week.
I could treat myself to something sweet without feeling guilty.
my boyfriend would surprise me with flowers.
I could have someone make great playlists for my iPod.
I could go back to that place in Mexico where I went with my
    family in college.
I could subscribe to all my favorite magazines.
I could take Italian lessons.
I could turn my shopping hobby into a business.
I could have a new plant in the house.
I could go somewhere exotic once a year.
I could learn more about wine.
I could have a baby in two years.
I could say "I love you" a little more easily.
I could eat out by myself without feeling strange.
I could buy more art.
I could read more fiction.

And so on . . .

This list is meant to get you in touch with your passions, your desires, and your enthusiasm for life. Pay careful attention to the small as well as the big things you want to accomplish. It's time to let your desires out and to be specific about what they are. The universe has a funny sense of humor, so a desire like "go somewhere hot this year" may translate into a job assignment on an isolated desert island rather than a romantic trip to Sardinia, so the more specific the better.

Once you've made your list, make an extra copy and put it where you can see it daily. The refrigerator, bedroom mirror, and the front door are all good places. Watch to see what happens, because your list is now *alive.* If you would like to accelerate the process, read your list to as many people as possible. Saying dreams out loud can be challenging for many women; it makes us feel vulnerable because we are so unfamiliar with the process of identifying *all* that we want. However, telling people about what you would like to experience is the first step toward achieving your big vision. You may get mixed reactions. Someone may challenge you by saying, "How do you plan on going to New Zealand if you want to have a baby next year?" Pay no attention to questions like this. Remember, this is not about how. Leave that to the universe to figure out for now.

Now that you've broadcast your desires to yourself and to anyone who you care to see or hear them, the secret is out! You've admitted that you would like a set of four-hundred-thread-count sheets, to learn how to change a tire, and to open a day spa, and it feels *good.* Getting your dreams out can bring a radical change. First, you will recognize that there are dreams you never knew you had. And second, you may find that it's not that hard to make something come true immediately, like magic. If this happens, the most important thing to do is to thank yourself, and whoever else is responsible, for making it happen. Even if it's a small thing, a thank-you acknowledges that you see the value in it and are ready for even more. If we don't acknowledge what comes to us, we don't send a signal to ourselves that the thing is important to us. So, should something suddenly get checked off the list, a big and heartfelt thanks is in order. It will be exciting to see how your list evolves and changes as time goes on. You may see something there that you no longer want, or watch how something you thought was unimportant becomes a priority. The list can be updated at any time, but we recommend keeping all lists, past and present, so you have a record of your desires and how they either happened or how your priorities changed over time.

Use the following questions to get further in touch with your launch project—they are designed to help you get to the root of your passion, to further understand yourself, and to gain deeper insight into your motivations. Make sure when you're answering these questions that you take some time for yourself, sit in a comfy chair, brew a cup of your favorite tea, put on a great album, light candles, and get into the mood to get to know yourself. You may be surprised and delighted with what you find out.

. . .

Portrait of a Lady

Heidi Keller came to the Incubator without any idea of what she wanted to do. She had a great job with an internationally popular sneaker brand and never had any thought or ambition to start her own business. Her top priority was going out, having fun, and meeting men. She enjoyed the Ladies Who Launch Incubator because it was a great place to meet other fun and motivated women . . . and to be social. In doing the workshop exercises, she began to zero in on her greatest passion (social circulating), which she had previously only regarded as a hobby. Going out and doing new things, meeting people, and making connections were her favorite things in life. More surprising was that it dawned on her that she'd had her fill of living in New York and she was ready to move west to be closer to her family and her childhood roots. To her amazement, within a month she sold her New York apartment, moved to Las Vegas where her parents resided, and started Get Out! Las Vegas. Her new business is a social club for single people that offers an alternative to planned singles events and traditional dating services; her business *embodied everything she was doing in New York, but that she was not treating as a serious passion. Getting in touch with her dreams and desires pointed her in a direction that she never would have imagined. She has successfully designed her life around her interests and passions, and now makes money doing it!*

Heidi's story demonstrates that being open and putting yourself in creative and motivating environments can lead to unexpected results. Unintended projects come barreling across your radar, and you may encounter opportunities you never dreamed possible. When answering the questions below, be as open as you possibly can.

Questions:

1. Close your eyes and breathe out and journey back to your earliest memory of playing. What did you love to do? Who did you like to do it with? Was it playing office or writing in your journal, dancing, or selling lemonade? What made you giddy and excited?

_____

_____

_____

2. Close your eyes and imagine $10 million is wired into your bank account (tax-free). After celebrating with a needed vacation and residential upgrade, what would you do? Would you quit your job? Would you move? How would your life be different from what it is now? Really picture it. Where are you and how do you spend your day? Who is in your life? What does your morning look like, and how do you end the day?

_____

_____

_____

3. Close your eyes and imagine that you are winning an award (Grammy, Academy Award, Nobel Peace Prize) or are being recognized

for something (Fast Company top 100, *Business Week* Philanthropy Issue). What would it be for?

_____

_____

_____

4. Name five people you most admire and why. If you could channel something from each of their lives (creative talent, family, lifestyle, job) what would it be? For example, Nicole Kidman for her grace and talent, Nancy Reagan for her love affair with Ronald, Bill and Melinda Gates for their partnership and philanthropy, Martha Stewart for her media empire.

_____

_____

_____

These exercises are designed to show you what is really important to you; your true passions. Do you notice any commonalities? Did you have any insights about yourself? A launcher is an explorer, always questioning, observing, and listening to the voices around her as well as her own. Connecting the dots about what makes you happy takes some interior engineering. It requires some quiet and candid thought. Let it marinate.

You want to make sure to incorporate what you have learned from the questions into your launch project. Here are some ways to interpret and evaluate the answers to the preceding questions.

1. How you played as a child is connected with your passion. You are born without filters and judgments. How you played is an indicator of your natural interests. Were you like Freya Williams, making your own homespun newspaper, who is now uncovering her passion for writing? Maybe you're like Amy Holbrook, who is an obsessive needlepointer and launched her business, AMH Design, which sells products for this craft? Looking backward is sometimes the first place to start in finding your way forward. Let your memories flow and enjoy reflecting on that little child who loved to play without boundaries or judgments.

2. Would your life be different with more money? If you answered no, congratulations, you are already living your passion. Oprah could have retired years ago with enough cash to fill the Grand Canyon, but she created a platform for herself that makes her so happy that she keeps doing it every day. Another ten million or even a billion wouldn't stop her from carrying out her dream on "The Oprah Winfrey Show." She would simply build more schools in Africa and have more to give away to charities and causes she supports. If you said that you would be living differently, we suggest you contemplate how you can start incorporating the changes that you would make now. For example, if more money would allow you to buy a new house, maybe you could consider a home project, or look at property, or perhaps venture in real estate? If you would quit your current job and become an organic farmer then joining a local co-op or cultivating your garden would be a step toward fulfilling your dream.

3. If your ultimate fantasy is to change the world so much that you win the Nobel Peace Prize, you want to make sure that your project involves taking a step in that direction. For example, you can volunteer with an organization whose mission is to eradicate AIDS or go to Africa to help create sustainable development. If your heart is in humanitarian concerns, check to make sure your path is headed in that direction, at least in one part of your life. If your dream is to win an Academy Award, your project might involve taking an acting class and performing in a play. The point is not to win these awards, very few people do . . . the point is that if you never get started you are guaranteed to never win the best award of all, which is a challenging, fulfilled life. Use your dream award as the ultimate guiding light to push your imagination and capabilities further . . . someone is going to do it, someone will win . . . so why not at least get in the game?

4. Compare and Inspire. It's fun and important to look at the world and think, "If she or he has it, then I can have it, too." If Julia Roberts has twins, then maybe I can. If Gwen Stefani can launch a clothing line, then I can do it. If Madonna can do a headstand in yoga, then I'll try. Also, what you admire in people is often an indication of what you desire for

yourself. It may feel like jealousy, but in this case it can be easily turned around to motivate you and get you to covet in a productive way. It's helpful to look to the world for inspiration, to see what there is to have and how others have accomplished what you also would like to achieve. We recommend looking at multiple sources; don't limit yourself to one role model or just women. You can easily stretch beyond five and take a little bit from as many as you can to create your own interesting mental collage.

Now that you've done some interior research, it's time to take this information from the exercises and write down the project that you would like to launch. Call it "My Project." And even if you aren't sure about what you want, take a stab and write as much as you can. More exercises throughout this book will help you to clarify, expand, and get your project out into the world.

> **Authors' Note:** Before you "declare" your project . . . People often ask us if we think there is anything that is a "bad idea" or a "stupid project." Our answer is no. We think that every idea, thought, or dream is something to be honored, treasured, and supported. You never know where an idea is going to lead you, so if you label it bad it is likely to lead you to a bad place and if you label it stupid then that means you think you yourself are stupid, because it was your idea. The way we look at it is that if your idea is to be a Tony Award–winning actress and all you ever do is take an acting class, then your life is already better. And who knows, you may meet your best friend in that acting class and start a bakery. So please try not to judge, evaluate, or criticize your project or dream; give it the love and nutrients that it deserves as a valued part of you.

Project Examples:

- I want to work from home and start a line of clothes that would allow women to feel comfortable whether they are working from home, exercising, going out at night, or running errands during the day. I want to use comfortable fabrics, soothing colors, and modern cuts.

- I am interested in finding happiness and fulfillment in a relationship. I want to find a life partner with whom to have children, take exotic vacations with, and to cook cozy dinners for. I also want to pursue a possible new venture in real estate development.
- I own a boutique graphic design firm. My project is to gain more substantial bread-and-butter revenue. I would like to attract bigger clients, while not sacrificing some of the smaller, creative ones whom I want to help as much as I can. I would like to develop a client base that is primarily comprised of larger, higher-paying clients.
- I want to open an event-planning business with a focus on children, and in particular, one with a tea party theme. I envision supplying games, tea, food, and creating costumes for fun characters, such as the Mad Hatter, for each child to wear. Maybe I would eventually branch out to other unique children's party themes as well.
- I want to keep my nine-to-five gig for now, but do something interesting on the side that uses my creative and business talents and also could be extra income. My project is to find this side endeavor. I don't know what it could be, but would like to know what my friends and family see for me.

Your project is merely a starting point or your launchpad. Recognize that with the input of others, this book, and your experiences, your project will grow, change, and evolve. In each of the following chapters you will rewrite your project, shaping it into what it will become. Projects are dynamic and these are yours. Take ownership and control of your dreams and get ready to launch!

It is time to write the first draft of your project:

_____

_____

_____

_____

_____

Congratulations. We know that for some this may be the very first time you've admitted this project to yourself, much less the world. Others may have thought about it, but didn't know how to develop it and help it grow. No matter what stage of the game you're in, now you can open the door to the Ladies Who Launch Incubator model. All you need to start launching is a dream, and now you've identified yours.

Destination One: Imagine It

The first destination of the Ladies Who Launch model is dreaming, imagining, and visualizing. You want to aim to create the biggest picture possible for yourself and your project. There is no room for playing small here! You don't have to. This is your spotlight and you want to turn it on full throttle, illuminating in detail your ideal work, perfect vacation, or the partner who would wholly complement you. Before we start, take a moment to consider how your life would be without imagination and dreams . . . or even fantasies. We don't want anyone questioning the value in dreaming! These dreams, exciting, crazy, or even scary, are the juices that keep life interesting and moving forward. Without aspirations to look forward to, we can lose our way and sink into a flat, uninspired mood. Conjuring thoughts of things that may not seem totally possible gives us a sense of movement and what-if? As a child, if you didn't have big dreams about dressing as you wanted to, spending your time as you wished, getting your ears pierced, or obtaining your driver's license, none of these activities would have felt like much of an achievement when you became a card-carrying adult. You appreciated these activities and achievements when they were just out of your reach because you thought about them over and over again. Those dreams fit the five-, ten-, or fifteen-year-old you were. Now you have new and bigger dreams, which possibly have more consequences. It's important to acknowledge these dreams, and not let anything get taken for granted. When you have access to your creative impulses and don't drown them in self-doubt, reasons why not, or negative thinking, you can exercise them so that they can come to a level of fruition either exactly as you imagined it, or in some way that may be different but better than you envisioned. You can decide that these are fun daydreams (but that you won't pursue them) or you can be like Leonardo da Vinci and imagine something that will happen hundreds of years in the future. Nothing is off-limits, or too small, too big, or too far out-of-bounds.

In the traditional model, the first step usually involves writing a business plan, producing numbers, figuring out an exact strategy for getting from point A to point B. Regardless of what your project is, whether a business, a hobby, or a new lifestyle, this model wants you to plan, crunch, and project.

The message in the traditional model is:

1. Don't think too big, especially if you don't know exactly how you will get there.
2. Stay focused on one thing. Don't deviate or divert your attention elsewhere.
3. Stay within a budget.
4. Make sure your time frame is accurate according to your numbers and production schedule.

There are merits to this approach; it's linear and sequential, and many a project has been completed by using it. The problem is, especially for women who are nonlinear thinkers, that if you are forced to analyze every potential idea for its true potential and consider all possible scenarios, there is a very good chance that you won't get started on anything. Giving yourself the freedom to imagine, without boundaries, during this stage of the process means not specifically calculating all the minutiae that go along with it. It doesn't mean that the minutiae aren't important! This is just the order of thinking we'd like you to use so that nothing gets in your way. Eventually we'll get to the part where we take action; but for now, let yourself be a kid again, and think as if anything is possible, just around the corner, or just a matter of time.

One benefit of putting reality checks aside (for the moment) and pretending that there is nothing limiting you from having every little bit of what you desire is that your brain operates in a different mode when it's free to explore. In other words, when it doesn't have to consider your bank account, education, age, your current schedule, or whatever has happened to you in the past, it can throw open the windows and let fresh air in that you may not have realized existed. Put anxieties aside, let go of your fears, and the trepidations that your friends and family may have for you. We ask that for once in your life you throw all caution to the wind and let your imagination breathe on its own, with no calculator attached.

Remember, everything that has ever been created has been imagined, by someone, somewhere. We bet that when Jennifer Lopez was a little girl she imagined being a superstar. Rosa Parks imagined sitting wherever she wanted to on the bus, whether this vision occurred minutes, days, or weeks before she did it. Cleopatra imagined being the queen who would save Egypt, and she enlisted the help of anyone she could. Posh Spice (Victoria Beckham) proclaimed as a youth that she wanted to be as famous as Persil (the top-selling British brand of detergent). Now *that* girl didn't have any limits at all! She could have said Madonna or the Queen of England, but she compared her future fame to something so common that no household in England is without it. These women did not feel the need to limit their imaginations and probably used their fears and resistances as motivation to go higher. Look at the results!

The Bigger You Dream, the Higher You Fly

Most of us, at one point or another in our lives, have gotten a well-intentioned (if a little corny) greeting card with the following message, "Shoot for the moon, and even if you miss, you will still be among the stars." Most of us have had the dreaming part of ourselves repressed (that's the shoot for the moon part), even crushed altogether. Maybe it was caused unintentionally by a parent, a teacher, or a friend who told you that you didn't have talent, your dreams were too much, too big, too crazy, wouldn't make money, or that dreams were reserved for "others" but not you. We learned to hold back because "being an actress is impractical," "there are already too many designers," "that's been done before," or "you should study something useful so that you can get a real job."

When you talk to true Ladies who have launched, they often cite childhood as the time when they first had thoughts about what they ultimately would do as grown-ups. As a child, Freya Williams started a newspaper with her best friend, with a promising circulation of one! Now she regularly writes articles for magazines. Another twenty-something Lady from Pennsylvania, Joan Snyder, used to play "boss" and advise her "employees" on achieving better results. Now Joan counsels girls graduating from college on career directions. Think back to some of the fantasy scenarios you used to play out and recall how nice it was not to have to feel as limited in your imaginings as you might now. You naturally gravitated toward something and did it. As a child, there were no limitations, your life was a blank slate, and you didn't care about your background, making money, or whether you were a girl or a boy, and you had no preconceived ideas about what society expected of you. We want you to get back in touch with this childhood place when anything and everything was possible. That child is still there within you, but you may not have talked to her for a while.

Embrace Your Resistance

When you think big and dream, resistance can come at you in a swarm. You imagine opening up your own store and suddenly you can think of ten reasons why this would be nearly impossible—nobody will come, you have no talent, you could go bankrupt, you'd be overly committed, and so on. If you dream about opening your own Pilates studio, suddenly you begin to think you have too little experience;

you've only been doing it yourself for a year, so why would anyone come to you. Many people would look at these objections or worries as reasons to stop and throw in the towel. While not everything deserves a green light, before making a decision, it's important to turn these thoughts around and embrace your hesitations. Seeing what you resist and acknowledging (in the light of day) what those things are is the first step toward overcoming them. In fact, if you embrace resistances, they can ignite creativity and make room for action. Exposing what holds you back ultimately makes you less fearful in general and opens you up to be more creative and confident in more than just one area of your life. Removing the obstacles can start an avalanche. There are usually one or two big boulders standing in the way of many thoughts and ideas. Targeting them (I'm not smart enough, I don't know anything about financing, I wouldn't know where to start, how would I even know how to raise a child) is the only way to move them. By pretending they're not there, our opportunities are limited because there is an undefined barrier to doing what we want to do. Barriers with no name can cause depression, anxiety, or a sense of hopelessness because when you don't know what's holding you back from your life, you can't do much to change it. Resistance can be emotional, physical, or financial. Women are amazingly resourceful and creative, and when they want something, nothing will stop them. The Taliban in Afghanistan, one of the most oppressive regimes in the world, couldn't completely halt the women it tried to undermine. Despite their reign of terror, they could not prevent women from finding a way to educate their girls in underground schools. In the face of paralyzing fear and dire consequences, women were able to do this and a great many other things, undercover.

To overcome resistance, you first have to pay attention to the "what" not the "how." With "what" anything is possible, with "how" you are constrained by trying to find one right way. Let yourself off the hook for a moment. If you want to move to the Caribbean and start a scuba-diving company, don't think about the job you'd have to give up, the house you'd have to sell, or the children you'd have to find schools for, simply think of the dream and all its possibilities. Imagine waking up in the morning in your thatched house by the beach, the mango you would prepare for your children for breakfast, the interesting people you'd meet while supplying scuba gear to adventurous travelers. Maybe you want to win on *Survivor* or buy out your boss, climb Mount Everest or read Proust's *Remembrance of Things Past* entirely in French. Don't focus on the negatives (you can't swim, you have ten dollars in the bank, you hate cold weather, or you failed seventh-grade French); you must dream as if there are absolutely no obstacles. Imagination creates the most infinitely sublime energy, where anything and everything your mind produces is actually possible. Accessing images and dreams has a strong impact on our lives and leads us toward that creative spark, inspiration, and vision where we begin to create. While we're sleeping, dreams are doing their creative work to filter ideas or explanations into your being, but dreams work in a very different way when you're awake. This part of the launching process is controlled dreaming. If you let your imaginative mind run free there is no telling where it will take you.

We love the story of Wangari Muta Maathai, founder of the Green-belt Movement, 2004 Nobel Peace Prize winner, biologist, professor, and now a Kenyan government minister. She rose to fame as a tree planter. Her aim was to rebuild her local economy and the environment in Kenya through rebirthing the forests that had been decimated by soil erosion and industrial development. She started by planting a few seeds in her own yard, and gradually, by sharing the idea with other women, got them to do the same. This movement started small but grew to be of international significance. There were serious hardships along the way. Maathai was so severely beaten during a governmental protest that she lost consciousness, and she continually faced intense criticism from Kenyan officials for decades before she received global recognition for her efforts. What a great example of a woman imagining something, harnessing other women to her cause, triumphing in the face of danger, and going on to be an official in a government that once wished she would disappear. Most of us don't face challenges this frightening. One seed at a time, she made a difference, and eventually built forests. One tree at a time, one woman at a time, she created a movement.

What If You Get Stuck?

Maybe you wonder, "Where is this process going?" Your ability to imagine may have petered out. It happens to all of us. Perhaps you want to get married, but you can't imagine walking down the aisle in the white dress, or you want to travel to Africa, but you only have two weeks vacation and a hefty serving of family obligations, or you want to launch an Internet company, but the term *Search Engine Optimization* is beyond your knowledge base. Fortunately, if you are having trouble, there's a way to kick-start your imagination that may surprise you.

If you can't imagine something that you desire happening, and someone else can imagine it for you, then it *is* possible. If you are stuck, it is time to pull out your natural resource that we talked about in chapter 3, your connecting ability. Often others can imagine much more for you than you can imagine for yourself because they are not limited by the fears and beliefs that hold you back. It's similar to wearing blinders that build over time, and you don't necessarily know what they are, just that they're there. Someone else won't see the same hindrances. The less they know you on a personal level, the less likely they are to see limitations on what you can achieve. Imagining for someone else is actually a great exercise in creativity. It's similar to decorating someone else's house with an unlimited budget—you might incorporate colors and unusual design elements that you would not attempt in your own home. In fact, if you think big and fantasize about bigger possibilities for others, you automatically start to expand your own mental territory. The saying "Birds of a feather flock together" holds true. People with big ideas, big dreams, and who undertake big actions tend to hang out in groups. Patti Smith, Bob Dylan, Robert Mapplethorpe, and Andy Warhol were peers in New York City, and all became famous for their artistry. You rarely see someone who has gone on to be incredibly successful continue to spend time with a group of friends who don't aspire to achieve much. Success is contagious. When one friend takes a big leap, goes for it, gets married, gets pregnant, launches a new company, or writes a book, others around her are inspired to do the same. Thinking big is infectious. If you're dreaming "big" for others, have a healthy appetite for your own world expanding, and make the effort to surround yourself with others who are supportive and share the same vision, you will all go higher because of one another.

. . .

Incubator Moment

Kris Mangano, a stunning forty-something living in Southern California, was aching to get out of her job as a corporate VP. For many reasons the position was no longer the right fit and she was exhausted by her schedule, which involved many days on the road traveling for gift shows. After observing so many women like herself who constantly traveled, she hatched an inventive way to help women travel more efficiently. Kris came to the Incubator hoping to leave her job someday and launch her own company. Her Web site would be designed to give women the tools they needed to travel, but streamlined to a few necessary items. The challenge would be to keep her bills paid, which meant staying in her job longer than she wanted, but which also meant much less time to create her business. One night, an Incubator leader from another city was visiting Kris's Incubator and began a conversation about Kris's job in the world of gift shows and sales/showroom reps. The leader asked Kris, "How could the women in my Incubator learn about all of the shows, when they need a rep, how to find one, and so on?" Kris thought for a moment, and hours later, had an epiphany. If she could leave her job and become a consultant to many young businesses that needed guidance in the gift arena, she could keep herself afloat financially and have time to start her company! By asking the right questions someone else had sent Kris into a direction she would not have thought of on her own. Ironically, Kris got laid off from her job and is now freelance consulting in the gift show arena while launching her travel accessory business.

It's remarkable what others can see for you, or lead you toward, that you would never conceive of for yourself. It's not that we don't want these great ideas to float our way, but often we have so many reasons why *not*, that we need someone else to pave the way a little bit. Or, we need a fresh perspective because we're too close to something. Getting input from others is the normal, wonderful, genius manifestation of the creation process. It can happen all the time, if you let it and are open to it. Below you'll find the first steps toward allowing others to see big things for you. Do the launchwork with an open mind, and by being a yes. The bolder and braver you are, the bigger the returns.

Launchwork

This series of exercises is meant to knock down the walls keeping your imagination captive so that you can dream bigger than you did yesterday. Ideas may rush toward you; fantasies you haven't entertained for years may suddenly resurface. Enjoy this process. There's hardly anything more fun than jamming to the tune of your own possibilities.

The fairy tale: for real. The first step is to write a story for yourself that details what will happen to you and your project. This isn't exactly fiction—it should represent the ultimate outcome of your vision. The key to the exercise is to step outside of yourself and pretend you are doing it for someone else and then think "best-case scenario." You want to turn off your "how" switch and only consider the "what." Dream away, and write it down.

Shannon's Project: "Expand My Business"

Shannon's project is to explore new ideas on how to advertise and expand Kartwheels Gymnastics, the business she owns in Cranston, Rhode Island. Shannon is deciding whether to divide her time between Kartwheels and teaching (utilizing her degree in elementary education and general science), which she loves, or choosing one career over the other. Shannon has a great opportunity to expand Kartwheels, as her landlord will soon be tearing down her current space, giving Kartwheels a brand-new building with a better look. One obstacle Shannon faces is the influx in her area of franchise gymnastic centers and their big advertising budgets. Not being part of a franchise gives Shannon the freedom to take Kartwheels in whichever direction she chooses. Shannon is looking for ideas on how to spread the word about Kartwheels, expand it, and gain knowledge and expertise in developing advertising and marketing tools in order to remain on top of the competition.

Here is her vision: "I just got back from the Olympics, where one of my girls won a gold medal. She started out at Kartwheels as a little girl, and went on to elite training as a young teen. Whenever she speaks, she always thanks me, Shannon, her first coach, for getting her started and helping her see what her true potential could be. After moving into my new space in 2007, I really took off, with enrollment that even had me surprised at what I could accomplish. I decided to franchise my concept, because so many people were calling and begging me to do it. I also brought in an ex-Olympic gymnast who was a huge draw and who became one of my star coaches. Kartwheels has become the premier training ground for young people interested in gymnastics, from the curious to the serious. Parents know that what their child gets here will teach them discipline, technique, and focus, but also fill them with the confidence to go out and do anything they want. I love having multiple locations and a business that fills kids with hopes and dreams."

Sharing the dream. Tell your dream to five of your friends, trusted colleagues, or acquaintances. This may seem awkward at first, but trust the process to reveal some interesting feedback. For the best results, choose individuals from an array of backgrounds, life experiences, age categories, and regions. Try to choose people to whom you feel closely connected as well as individuals to whom you feel less connected or know less well. The more diverse and dynamic the group, the better you will maximize the effects of this exercise. Ask them to write or tell you a scenario that gives life to what they see for you based on what you've told them. Reassure them that this is not something that involves a to-do list or advice from them on "how" to do it. You want them to be free to just let their imaginations go, and tell you what it is they see. They can also include themselves, as if the dream has happened, as in, "Alison calls me to announce that 'The Oprah Winfrey Show' has called and is featuring her story."

For an extra-credit bonus exercise, for people who really want to dive in, do the same for them. Ask what their project is and imagine something for them. Not only is this a great exchange, but it will unleash your own creativity and have you thinking in big ways for each other. You will be very surprised at what different people say about you. Notice how it feels to ask for someone's help (this can be difficult, although most people will be excited to be a part of your process), and also pay attention to what those who know you well, versus those who don't, see for you.

Melissa's Project: "My Project Is to Get Married."

Melissa has decided she is going to focus on getting married. Melissa had come to believe that marriage was probably something that she could not have. Her new project is becoming a woman who can "have" marriage.

Friend's vision for Melissa: "I was so happy that Melissa let us choose our own style of bridesmaids' dresses, in such a beautiful color. The whole wedding was feng shui'd down to the color of the dress. I am so proud as I watch Melissa dance with her new husband. She seems so calm, confident, and in love. My husband and I spend many weekends with them out at the beach and in the mountains skiing. They are so much fun to hang out with. Melissa is now doing her own projects, which include a combination of workshops, feng shui, and other creative endeavors. She is also enjoying planning her weekends in the country with her husband, and preparing for a new arrival."

Gina's Project:

"I Need Distribution and Support for My Inhale-Exhale Guide." Gina is looking to expand her Inhale-Exhale Guide, a resource for sports, fitness, beauty, and wellness, possibly launching it in different cities. She is looking for distribution and assistance.

One friend's vision for Gina: "Whenever I travel, I make sure that I check out the inhale-exhale Web site, where I can find listings for yoga, Pilates, and massages in every city. It is also helpful because people go online and rate the different programs, so you can get a good idea of what will be a quality class and a good fit. Inhale/Exhale is in every major city and gets more advertisers each year. Gina eventually left her job to focus on this full time and has her own Inhale/Exhale studios around the country."

Another friend's vision for Gina: "Gina decided to adopt the Zagat's model of corralling different 'testers' in every city to give her the inside scoop on new classes, offerings, studios, and workout facilities. These testers were considered key marketing strategists and were able to give her critical information about regions she would otherwise lose track of. They also spearheaded events in each city to promote the guide. Soon, all of their friends wanted to be testers as well, as the guide rose to international prestige and included European locations. Soon Paris, Rome, Budapest, Berlin, London, and many other cities were added."

Kenyetta's Project: "Find Investors and Salespeople for Butterfly Kisses."

Kenyetta is building a multilevel marketing company around her line of beauty products, Butterfly Kisses. She needs to find investors and to bring other salespeople on board to represent and sell the line.

One friend's vision for Kenyetta: "Kenyetta stands on a podium in front of a hundred sales associates in a glamorous ballroom at the St. Regis Hotel in New York. It's so great to see the enthusiasm and excitement for this new, totally natural bath and body line, which has now become a household name. I meet Kenyetta over a quick break to introduce her to someone from QVC who wants to sell her line as a package starting that fall. Butterfly Kisses is soon in the bathrooms of women everywhere, especially since the airing of her infomercial explaining the importance of chemical-free beauty products."

Another friend's vision for Kenyetta: "Kenyetta has found a retail location in West Hollywood big enough to include not only her own products, but those of other Incubator members. She brings together a collage of different products under one roof, and gives everyone a chance to have a brick-and-mortar retail experience. Kenyetta decides that New York City should be the next location for one of her boutiques, and then Chicago. These stores are made up of all women-owned businesses and give owners a place to showcase their wares and have easy distribution channels."

Questions for Reflection

After doing these exercises, do you feel that your vision for your
project has expanded?

Do you feel clearer about what it is that you want to do?

Do you find validation in the visions that your friends imagined
for you?

Are there aspects of the visions you never thought of before,
solid ideas that you can see yourself implementing?

Are you surprised or elated or made uncomfortable by any of
the visions created for you? Are you scared or fearful (this is
okay and actually a common response to receiving a lot of
input) about what would happen if these visions came true?

Has visioning or imagining for others impacted the evolution
of your own project?

Remember the freedom that this process encourages and bring it into
your everyday life. "How" you can achieve your dreams will become
important in the future, but we are tireless in our campaign for ignit-
ing wild and rambunctious imaginations, and know that the "what"
must come first!

Keep these visions in a safe place so that you can refer to them often, or incorporate them in any and all materials you may create for
your project as you move through the launching process.

Destination Two: Speak It

Now that you have accumulated others' visions for you and your project, you are armed with a treasure chest of creativity and fresh perspectives, not to mention the energy of those around you.

Step two of the Incubator process is to speak it! Once you've imagined something, saying it out loud makes it more real. In chapter 8 you were exploring, imagining, and soliciting the visions of others in order to arrive at a clearly defined project. Now, articulating the scope of this project to as many people, and in as many different environments as possible, increases the likelihood of positive action toward your dream. You can think all day, all week, or all year about a hobby, dream, goal, or business you'd like to delve into, but until you talk about it, you're much less accountable. By projecting and communicating a clear vision and message, you pave the road for further action and bring others (the listener) into your community, whether they become a part of its actualization or not. Once words escape your lips into the receptive ears of another human being, what was once a lonely voice in your head is now a formulated, debatable, accepted, rejected, or more literal aspiration.

While driving home from the dentist, the grocery store, the vet, or a date, have you ever had a brilliant idea that seemed completely possible, only to wake up the next morning to the reality of it? Maybe you considered a move to China to take advantage of its opening market, with the afterthought that you would miss your family too much. Perhaps you imagined giving up everything for a relocation to Aspen to become a ski instructor, or to Bali to export handbags, then realized it was simplification you were craving, not necessarily a ski town or island life. Conjuring and then rejecting ideas is the natural editing process your mind goes through when it evaluates information and then decides if it's either worth something or not. Self-doubt also factors into the process. How do you discern between a legitimate rejection of an idea versus a self-limiting doubt? You check your intuition for fear and you check the longevity of the dream. If a thought or idea plagues you for long enough, and you aren't doing anything about it, it's usually because fear is keeping you stapled to a life that's a safer bet. And guess what? Sometimes safe is okay! A single mom has fantasies about living in a remote village and raising her child away from television, pop culture, pollution, and crime. Does she do it? Maybe she doesn't because she has a well-paying job that keeps a nice roof above both their heads and pays for a prestigious school for her child, but she books a four-week stay in a mountain cabin for the summer. Or, maybe she does leave because whatever exists in her current life isn't enough to hold her back from picking up and getting in a car to "somewhere." She may experience fear no matter which decision she makes, but true desire will squash doubt if it's strong enough and has been simmering long enough.

Doubt keeps us from talking about so many thoughts and ideas. When embarking on a dream it is common for our internal voice to pipe up and say, "What if people think I'm crazy? What if my friends don't get it? What if I say something and then someone tells me it's not possible?" Many people, especially women, don't talk about new projects or ideas because they feel they need to be proven first. Step two of the Incubator process is so scary because speaking a dream out loud to friends, family, or strangers forces you to consider whether or not it is viable and whether you will have the courage to go for it.

Remember, saying it doesn't mean committing to it. You could simply muse about possibilities: "Sometimes I dream of moving to Aspen and teaching people to ski all day long," or "I wonder about moving to China and taking advantage of the booming economy." Saying it exorcises it. It gets it out, but what will come of it no one can really tell. Perhaps a friend is going to Shanghai on a business trip and invites you to go with her, and a business-exploration trip is born. You may encounter someone who was a ski instructor in Sun Valley who has some useful information about what that life entails. Saying your dream or vision out loud may simply bring you more information to factor into your plans. Do with it what you want, but in order to discover anything, you gotta talk about it!

There are three important components of the speak it stage:

1. Articulating your internal vision. You may understand the idea inside of you, but until you actually say it out loud, and to another person, you won't know if what you're saying makes sense. This is a good test.

2. Finding your own unique voice means getting used to saying what it is you do (or want to do), and allows you to start to feel authentic about it. It's easy to feel like a fraud at first. When the words "I'm a writer" come out of your mouth and all you've done is write poetry in a secret binder kept under the bed, you will feel a little uncomfortable. Get used to it. You'll be no more of a writer if you get those poems published or continue your private habit. If you write, and that's something you do, then you can be a writer. You have to find your voice and find your "skin" about it.

3. Talking about your vision will invite a variety of reactions (whether solicited or not) from others that you can either choose to pay attention to, incorporate, or ignore.

Expressing Your Vision

Verbalizing thoughts is a way to process them or get to the essence of something. When an idea is lodged inside us, sometimes speaking about it is one of the scariest things we can do. Women often say, "If

I talk about it then I have to do something about it!" By taking the risk and overcoming the fear, you let the creation process build momentum. Stacey, a thirty-something-year-old mom and owner of a hugely successful consulting business in Los Angeles, had a dream of taking her business to the next level. She often referred to this next level in class but had not decided what that level was, or what she meant by it. She said she had goals to expand all over the country, not just in Los Angeles, and she also spoke of being a household brand name. When Stacey left class and began to do her homework, which was to move forward by telling people about her expansion ideas, she had a major epiphany. As she talked about it, she realized she wasn't clear about what she wanted. In hearing herself articulate her goals to friends and associates, she realized that to become the brand name she wanted to be, she needed to figure out what made her business different. She had to define her brand equity; the thing that set her consulting firm apart from anyone else's and gave her creation value beyond her personal contribution to it. How could it stand on its own without her there to tend to its upkeep? The company could only thrive if there was a formula that could be replicated anywhere, and without her personal management of it. She thought the launchwork would be easy for her because she talked about growing her business to the next level all the time. The launchwork helped her think about what that next level meant, and she discovered while trying to speak it that she had to build her brand further and discover its core qualities first. If Stacey hadn't been pushed to speak it, it might have taken months or years to discover what she really wanted to do. A seemingly easy task had a transformative effect on Stacey and her business.

. . .

Incubator Moment

Amy Schuber left a corporate job that made her miserable to determine what she wanted to do next. She had begun to dabble in sewing, and had developed a pattern for making baby blankets using vintage fabrics. Initially, making blankets was just a hobby that benefited a few of her friends who had re-

cently had babies. As Amy began to see her work as a viable business, she joined the Incubator to put some momentum behind it. When it came to speaking it, Amy found that she no longer asked people what they thought of what she was doing, as she had in the past. As she spoke to those around her about the blanket business she expressed herself using statements, instead of questions. When she reported back to class about this slight shift in her thinking, she had a revelation. She no longer cared what everyone thought! It mattered more what she thought, and in having to go out and speak it, she understood more fully her own commitment to her business and officially launched Pickle Princess. This was a great moment for Amy because from that week forward her confidence soared to new levels. She was no longer asking for permission, she was enthusiastically spreading the word without a shadow of doubt that she had found the right path.

· · ·

Incubator Moment

*E*sther *was a New York transplant living in Los Angeles. In her mid-thirties, she'd enjoyed a busy and rich social life in Manhattan before relocating for a job that kept her on the road more than 50 percent of the time. She was deeply unhappy with her job, and also frustrated with the lack of time she was able to spend cultivating a new life in California. Esther joined an Incubator to quite literally "get a life." Shortly after her Incubator started, she left her job and moved into something new that didn't involve travel. Through listening to different women in her Incubator and also to herself speak, she made an announcement during week three: "I've decided something," she said. "I now live in L.A." The room broke up with laughter because although she'd been living in L.A. for more than a year, she hadn't decided it was her town yet. With this proclamation came an effort on her part to reach out to others, which in turn prompted phone calls, invitations, dinner plans, and parties in return. Esther finally consciously made a move to build her life, instead of waiting for her New York life to follow her west.*

Another outcome of expressing your internal vision is that by letting information out into the world you're making it possible for others to play a role in helping or supporting your cause. People can't really help you if they don't know what it is that you are imagining. Speaking it gives everyone a way to connect or contribute, in a way that they wouldn't have if you hadn't invited them in. One woman launching a line of cosmetics found it paralyzing to talk about her project outside of her Incubator group. She'd been brave enough to join, but that was as far as she was comfortable going. When told of the homework to speak her project to five people, she recoiled. She was fearful not only of public speaking, but also of people stealing her idea. Feeling proprietary is a conundrum many entrepreneurs face that carries mythic baggage you can either accept or reject. Some say speaking about an idea before it's a done deal can blow the whole thing before it gets off the ground. It can let the steam out and allow it to be overdiscussed before it's been executed. We disagree with that and feel that by talking about ideas, you actually allow the world around you to help you move those ideas forward faster. The cosmetics gal worried about someone using her idea or overanalyzing it, but when she reported back to the group, her tune had changed. She found that by speaking it, she learned how to talk about her project in a way that invited someone to come forward as a possible investor. Had she kept this idea secret and close to the vest, no one would have been able to discern that she needed help, financially or otherwise. By following the exercise, she attracted a young finance guy who is interested in her project and possibly in a partnership.

Developing Your Unique Voice

The truth is that there is nothing new in the world. What ends up making a new product successful is something unique about the packaging or positioning; taking something that already exists and making it smaller, brighter, or distinctive. You may create a new color, a new concept, or develop a new take on an old thing, but the world is big and chances are that someone else has probably already done something similar. We don't mean to discourage you, but only to drive home the point that the best thing about you or your project is *you* and your spin on it. Only you can present it, defend, it or manifest it in the way that you have dreamed it. You are the package, which is why your package needs to be considered. If Coca-Cola had poured some carbonated sugar water into paper cups and sold it on the street, it would have been fairly indistinguishable from any other company that had a similar product. But Coca-Cola created a product, songs, and a name that is recognized internationally. Branding is beyond the scope of this book, but in finding your own voice, sometimes it helps to look at yourself just as a company would look at itself.

Think about Stevie Nicks, Sheryl Crow, or Annie Lennox. Each has a very unique style, from the clothes they wear to their hair and makeup to their actual sound. Your project will have its own characteristics. Sometimes we know our own projects so well that we feel paralyzed when trying to articulate them to others. At times, we're just beginning to understand what we want to do and feel fearful and hesitant to talk about something at such an early stage. These are legitimate and very common complaints about the speaking stage; however, your listeners will act as a mirror and sounding board in a way that you cannot provide for yourself. They give us signals and feedback that shape ideas and often become integral players in how our visions unfold. The most important aspect of speaking your vision, however, is your voice.

Your voice is how you express yourself verbally or otherwise. It includes your body language, the way you shake someone's hand, the many ways in which you interact with people socially or professionally, and includes the way you dress, how you write an e-mail, how you speak on the phone, and how you respond to criticism. Sometimes it takes months to find the voice that feels the most authentic for you. But it is very hard (if not impossible) to find it without another person listening. Once you share an idea, even if it's in the infant stages and you know you're only at the tip of the iceberg, people will let you know what is clear, and what is not, about your message. For example, if the receiver of your message follows or responds positively, you know your message is being heard or articulated well. We call this "good reception," your signal is coming in clearly. If the listener is confused, misunderstanding you, or totally disinterested, it's a fair indication that you are unclear about your message and need to either refine your presentation, tweak or change your idea, or assume that you don't have an interested audience. On the bright side, even a bad audience can be good practice. Even rock stars don't have a perfect reception every time they perform, especially early in their careers. Refining your voice and what you say can be a clumsy process, but that's okay. One of the ways we learn to talk about new ideas is by testing them and seeing what the best way to talk about them is. Letting fear or doubt get in the way blocks the process.

Embracing Feedback

It's easy to think that other people are the problem if they don't understand your idea or concept. This is usually not the case. If one person doesn't get it, then there are probably one hundred or more like them who also won't get it. Your personal responsibility is to present your vision in a way that makes sense. You not only need to understand and create your voice, but also deliver the information in the best and most original way possible. If you wait for the listener, buyer, or even your family members to make all the effort to understand your very clear vision that lies only in your imagination, you might remain frustrated for a long time. Once you share your ideas, you will get many forms of feedback. Sometimes it will be negative and sometimes it will be critical. There is a big difference between "negative" and "critical." Negative feedback is judgmental. It doesn't look at the project from the perspective of what the strengths and weaknesses might be, it only puts it down without substantiating why. Critical feedback may have good information in it because, whether you agree with it or not, it's based on a point of view. Getting critical points of view will actually force you to get to know your market, your plan, or your product even better. Thank people who are critical! They are doing you a service by showing you what to look at. However, judgment and negativity have no place in the creation process, and don't belong in your universe. Thank those negative people for their thoughts, but keep moving. When you put yourself out into the world you are bound to encounter negativity in some form, so don't be surprised and prepare yourself to handle it. Creativity and new ideas can be threatening to others, and it's up to you to surround yourself with people who will offer their honest opinions combined with support and love. But understand that love may look like criticism, too. Some of our most successful Featured Ladies were told by others close to them that their ideas were crazy or that they would never work. Many people (men) told Liz Lange that women would not spend money on beautiful maternity clothes; they were fine wearing their husband's big shirts. But Liz Lange and others persevered with their visions anyway and in many cases achieved success beyond their wildest dreams. That's not to say that feedback, if done constructively, should be wholly ignored. Look for a consistent message. Is everyone telling you that your educational product would be better suited as a service or that the name you are thinking about for your marketing consulting company sounds like a child's play toy? Sometimes an idea might need to be tweaked or changed, or a new direction taken. It is up to you and your intuition that we cultivated earlier in chapter 5 to decide. You are best served by recognizing any resistances you might have and by remaining as open as possible throughout this process. Many women join the Ladies Who Launch Incubator to find people who will tell them the truth in constructive and supportive ways.

The greatest idea in the world can easily get buried in a muddled pitch, a confusing story, or a nervous or shy presentation. Imagine your idea not taking off because no one could hear you, or because your demeanor communicated a lack of interest or confidence! What a shame and waste that would be.

If You Say It, It Will Come (Or at Least Is More Likely To!)

There is power in saying something out loud. We aren't suggesting you share every waking thought with those around you, but for those things you need action on, speaking it can sometimes cause motion.

Have you ever noticed that when you need something and casually mention it to someone in passing, they often have a solution for you, even when there is seemingly no connection whatsoever between what you need and the receiver of the information? A woman checked her voice mail while at her local gym and while listening to a message from a doctor complained to another woman that she could never get an appointment. They spoke briefly and the first woman was immediately connected to the second woman's husband, a well-known M.D. While some may consider this a lucky coincidence or a lucky break, we'd like to offer another take on it. When you're in the flow of your life, and you allow the world to support what you need, you make it much, much easier for "luck" to happen. Luck thrives in certain environments, and your goal is to optimize yours so that it can make regular appearances.

If you apply this concept to talking about a project or business, imagine what can happen. People usually want to connect and help, and it won't take much asking for them to volunteer information or assistance. The goal of speaking it is not necessarily to elicit a response from anyone who hears you, however. It's simply using the process as a sounding board and seeing what happens. Does your message land? Are you feeling more comfortable talking about your project? Each time you talk about it is an opportunity to test it a little further and to hone your voice. The benefit may be a great connection, suggestion, or inside information on the next hot sample sale! Talking up your project can reap great rewards.

Launchwork

The exercises in this chapter are designed to help you get your project out into the world and to listen and shape your voice by practicing on a variety of people, including those who know you best, acquaintances, or even someone you meet for the first time.

Speak it, believe it. Now, it's time to talk about your project! Tell ten people you come in contact with over the next week or so about what you are working on. See how it feels to talk about it. See how they respond. Use these opportunities to experience your new identity, if it is one, or to explore and play with something different. Most important, have fun! Many people doing this exercise have felt everything from fear, excitement, shame, joy, and exuberance while talking about their projects. Pay attention to how you feel, how it goes, and go for it! You could talk to your mom, your local coffee barista, or someone you meet a cocktail party. Just look around . . . there's always someone to tell. If you like, explore the Ladies Who Launch online community and reach out to women who might have projects or ventures that are synergistic with yours!

Describe yourself. Ask five people to come up with two to three adjectives or positive words to describe you. This is an important exercise and might be the most difficult to implement because these words express the essence of you, and that is what will infuse your project. Some may choose to describe you in terms of famous people (Oprah meets Madonna), or some might describe you in a nutshell as the type of person you are (supermom diva), or they might simply use adjectives (sensitive, determined, artistic). Feel free to provide them with these examples to explain the exercise. After you receive the information, ask yourself: are you surprised by their descriptions or do they simply confirm what you already knew? Are there aspects of their descriptions that you are thrilled about, or are they things that you wish to change? Are there commonalities among their descriptions? Pay attention, as you'll want to note if four out of five people described you as "artistic" or "organized." Are you in agreement with their perceptions of you? If not, why not? If yes, are you comfortable with their perceptions?

Example:
   Victoria: "Visionary, life launcher." "The reason I go back to this description is that it makes it clear, throughout my day, as I drive Ladies Who Launch to new places, that this is who I am and what I do. This is my reminder."
   Beth: "Cool friend." "Someone gave this to me in my first Incubator and it always stuck with me because I never wanted to be perceived as a 'coach' or 'guru' per se; I always wanted to be approachable and like a cool friend that you can always rely on and count on."
   Amy: "Golden scribe." "I love this description of me because whenever I doubt my abilities or question what I should be doing with

my life, it reassures me that working with words is my strength and identity. This helps me remember that."

This is an important exercise because once you have a clear understanding of your internal voice, you will be able to carry this identifier through all of your projects, creative endeavors, and life pursuits.

Pulling it all together. Now that you have practiced putting yourself out into the world, you have the feedback and insight to craft what is known as an elevator speech. If you've never heard this term, it refers to the idea that you want to be able to get your message across in the time it takes to ride an elevator—about eleven seconds. If you don't ride a lot of elevators you could call it a picking up the kids from school speech, a dropping off your dry-cleaning speech, or even a getting a latte at Starbucks speech.

The standard elements to a perfect pitch are as follows:

Who am I? As in, "Hi, I'm Jen Sincero."

What do you or your company offer? "I am a writer."

After this, ***identify the problem you solve and the main contributions you make* (your clients or customers, or the service you provide).** "I write a weekly column for men and women about relationships and sex called 'Living in Sin' and am writing a screenplay for a major cable network based on my book *Don't Sleep with Your Drummer.*"

If you have a business that requires more explanation, you could also ***tell them how it is you work with them,*** for example, "I sell my products through an online store," or "I work with individuals and families to find resolutions to conflict."

Finally, and if you have time, you might add one sentence that distinguishes you from anyone else who might be doing something similar to what you are doing and gives the listener one action or one question they could answer.

Examples:

"I make talking about sex funny and entertaining. Do you have any questions you'd like to ask?"

"We offer everything from the one and only patented handbag

hanger to laptop carryalls. Do you have any favorite boutiques or stores? I'm always looking for them."

Here are a couple more examples in their entirety.

"My name is Henri Hebert and I cofounded FiveFold Productions with my producing partner, Kimberly Goodman. We create content for documentaries, television, feature films, and commercial projects that do everything from entertain to educate."

"My name is Miki Shaler and I cofounded Zen Baby. We created a DVD for infants and parents designed to create a calming environment in the home. Do you know any new parents? This would be a great gift."

Practice your pitch using your own information and all the feedback you received. Don't just leave it on a piece of paper. Go out and practice! If people respond by wanting to help or by asking questions, you know that you had "good reception," if not, it just means you might need to do some fine-tuning.

By the time you've finished this homework, you will have a flurry of thoughts about your project and possibly some great movement to report. Speaking it really stirs the pot, so hang on to your purse straps and enjoy the ride.

10
·········

Destination Three: Do It

Now it's time to put your brilliant plot into action. This chapter will help you get off your couch (the mental or the literal one) and get into action toward achieving your vision, project, goal, or idea. Whenever you take a grain of an idea and start taking action to make it happen, a new version of yourself can begin to emerge. Old identities and fears start to fade, and a new and more interesting person takes form. Once you ignite the flame of your true passion, you will be amazed by what and who comes toward your new light. Once you've begun forming a vision and are working toward developing your voice, you need to take action to make them real. If you are starting a business, you may have to get counsel from an accountant or lawyer about forming an S Corp, a Limited Liability corporation, or perhaps your endeavor doesn't require any incorporated structure. But it's important to ask. If you are a single mom launching your social life, you might have to find a babysitter who can be more spontaneous and flexible to accommodate your new schedule. If your dream is to be an opera singer, you may need to research local opera companies or sign up for voice lessons. You need to find the optimal conditions for what you want to do by laying the pavement. We're helping you harness your motivation and energy, inspiring your forward movement, and then showing you how to create the support system that will help you turn your dream into the reality that we know it can and should be.

It's amazing what can happen when a focused, potent dose of attention is put toward a goal. With any dream, after imagining it and speaking it, you have to do it.

A great mind once said, "Success is preparation meeting opportunity." If you walk down the street in old sweats and a T-shirt and run into a hot guy or potential client, you won't be prepared for the opportunity. On the other hand, if you leave the house feeling totally gorgeous and together, and happen to run into this same contact, you're prepared for something successful. You've done the prep work and now it's time to take action. Or, let's say you've been dragging your feet on updating your Web site and in the meantime get a fantastic piece of press or potential investor. If the Web site isn't in good shape, you're not ready for those opportunities.

Sometimes when we talk about taking action women think that we mean to work hard or to do more tasks. You've probably heard "nobody gets anywhere without hard work" and while this can be true, we've been taught to do the work in a way that doesn't use our intuition or our ability to create entire networks to support our feminine voices. In the traditional model, doing tasks equals more success. When we say get into action we are not talking about hard work because when you are launching something you've developed from your passion, it doesn't feel like work. Of course some things will feel tedious and not fun, such as setting up a postal account or refilling the printer cartridge, but when you're making progress doing something important and exciting for you, it doesn't carry the same baggage that traditional work does. If you're going to take on activities that bring you joy or just get the job done the first step is to get moving.

Whether you have more than one hundred employees or only one, are in a position to hire a PR agency or rely on word-of-mouth, retain an event planner or do it yourself, ultimately, the success of whatever you are launching is up to you. It is going to come into being because of the passion, vision, and energy that you put into the project. However, while nobody is going to do it for you, you can get a lot of help by outsourcing and delegating. Taking action flips the switch that gets your project off the ground.

. . .

Portrait of a Lady

Gigi Chang, founder of Plum Organics, a line of frozen organic baby food that provides a real food alternative to jarred baby food, drew on her and her husband's assets as well as funds from immediate family to make a substantial investment in her company to conduct extensive focus groups, hire a top branding company, and develop her product. But it was her passion, commitment, and determination to get her product launched within a narrow time frame that ultimately made her dream into a successful reality. After identifying consumer research, brand development, and product development as three areas in which she wanted to invest, Gigi did something that was almost unheard of in the industry—she focused on each of these areas simultaneously in order to push her idea forward faster. Gigi lived her passion for feeding children healthy food in her own life—she was constantly creating organic, all-natural baby food and freezing it, and became known for her creative, healthy, and appealing baby food concoctions. She imparted her enthusiasm to all her team members—as a result, her branding experts, product developers, and research specialists all became driven on her behalf to launch her products and get them on store shelves by the summer of 2006. Without her energy and unrelenting attention to her project, she may have been overshadowed by the competition, or worse, her idea may never have gotten off the ground. Plum Organics is now available in Wild Oats, Whole Foods, and natural grocery retail stores nationwide.

Break It Down

It's fun to imagine how you will spend all of the money you make from your amazing idea, plan your Oscar speech, or plot your takeover of daytime talk shows after Oprah retires. But once the fun stops and the planning should start a lot of people get stuck because they get over-whelmed by *everything* that they have to do—the proposal, the meetings, the financing, the office space, the future staff, and all the steps that they have to take to make their vision a reality. What's important is to set your priorities and learn from the way others have done it. You have to consult the experts. Read everything you can on what others have done and see what makes sense for you. Inside the Ladies Who Launch Incubators there are many experts who are willing to share their stories and experiences with new members that often people don't have to look (or pay) for this advice; it's right in front of them or only an e-mail away. But all of your questions cannot be answered by one person, so you will want to utilize the people in your life to forge the path. Ask your uncle who manufactures accessories why he produces in downtown Los Angeles versus China. Ask your cousin, a bookkeeper, if QuickBooks is the best way to keep track of your money, and if she could spend a couple of hours teaching you how if you make her a fabulous dinner. Enlist your friendly neighbor to help you with research and your best friend to see if there is anyone else out there doing what you're doing. Call on your unofficial team to help you; chances are, people will help. But you have to ask, and be prepared to reciprocate with a batch of fresh cookies, something you can offer as a skill, or even a beer after a long day.

The trick is to prevent the paralysis before it sets in, and not to think that everything has to be done right now. If you take one step, then another and another, before you know it you will be where you want to go. Many women complain that "It never seems to end!" and this can seem true. In the business building stage, it's an unraveling story, so thank goodness it *isn't* ending. We've learned that by breaking bigger tasks into smaller ones—taking on your jobs in bite-size pieces—not only do you stand a better chance of getting something done, you'll be able to feel a sense of accomplishment every day you have checked one task off of your to-do list.

Nobody ever got anywhere overnight. When pressed, the most suc-cessful people out there will say they still think of themselves as the dreamer with a crazy idea or the kid in college yearning for something more.

Sometimes Action Means Slowing Down

Are you frantic, hectic, or sprinting between one task that never seems to end and a list of others with little progress? Does one day blur into the next, with breathless meals in between? Sometimes extremely busy people need to slow down before they can move forward. It may seem counterintuitive, but even sitting on the couch for thirty minutes with a magazine or TV show can be rejuvenating or a "brain nap." Being too full, overscheduled, manic, and crazed does not (ever) foster your best creativity. Breakthrough ideas or problem-solving revelations don't often come in the midst of chaos. We can't speak for everyone, but our studies and observations, as well as personal experience, tell us that when you are overloaded, the best you can do is react. When you're reacting to what's coming at you, there's much less room to create or to allow the creation process to blossom. It's easy to feel that if you don't return a call, do a household project, or attend an event the world (as you know it) will end. The truth is that you're losing out by bouncing from one thing to another. Nothing gets your full attention. Considered, thoughtful action is very challenging in this state, so take a break, slow down, lie on the couch, go on vacation, or escape the race for a moment. If you are running through life, you're moving too fast to build anything and not moving slowly enough to know what to build! For many busy women, simply watching TV or sitting on a lawn chair reading a magazine brings on guilt, but brilliance happens when you make room in your life for ideas to enter. For now, see what you can edit. You can always reincorporate it later; but if there is any way to reduce your stress and obligation, do it. Find an extra set of hands somewhere, if they exist, and enlist them.

Take time for that indulgence that others might label as wasting time. Read a trashy novel, go to the movies in the middle of the afternoon, spend the whole day in pajamas, leave the dirty dishes in the sink, hang out in a café all day, or visit with friends who drop by. Sometimes you need those days, weeks, or even months when there is nothing "productive" happening so that you can gain the strength and desire to be creative and productive again. It will feel good when you get back to it. We don't consider taking a breather a waste of time. It's an opportunity to recharge your batteries and open yourself up to opportunities and ideas you might miss if you are constantly on the go. Even women who are juggling kids with work can schedule a massage and be disciplined about sticking to it, and even just a scheduled time-out on the bed with an iPod can help.

People can also get stuck because they are in such a hurry to make things happen that they don't listen to their intuition about the next steps they should take. Sometimes intuition knows a lot more than you do. The key is to be awake enough to hear and pay attention to it when it's communicating with you. Have you ever noticed that a dream can sometimes inform a plan or notion that you've been brewing up? Or how a walk between the grocery store and dry cleaner may allow you to see something that inspires a brilliant epiphany? When you move too fast it creates imbalance and the organic process of creation cannot fully be realized.

Sometimes we think we want something to happen much faster than we are prepared for, physically and emotionally. Have you ever heard a girlfriend complain that she can't seem to find a good guy? That there are no great men out there and that all she seems to attract are losers? You couldn't introduce her to a great guy in her current mode of thinking because as much as she thinks she's ready, she is still focused on the negative. If you did get a nice guy in front of her, she would not know how to attract him. She isn't prepared for a good guy because she's still entertaining the less-than-great ones. Once she sees a good man in her life, in any way, she will be much more prepared to see others. For example, Julia dreamed of launching a clothing brand, but had let it idle for years. A former model, she'd spent her time on sets, on locations in exotic cities, and around racks, and racks, and more racks of clothing for more than a decade. She joined the Incubator to better understand what type of brand she wanted to launch, and how she could best use her experience as a model to create it. At week three in the Incubator, she'd found an investor for her idea. By week four she had a name, a checking account for the business, a trade show under her belt, and was off to a blazing start. She wondered if all of that time she was idling was a waste and that maybe her business could have taken off much earlier. The truth is, she realized that she would not have been mentally and emotionally prepared earlier, nor would the perfect investment partner have been available. It's important to trust that things will happen at the exact time that you can actually handle them.

Making It Happen

Now is the time to draw on your more traditional masculine side, the one that's results oriented and makes things happen. We told you that we would circle back around to this important part of you, the part that makes things happen. The key is to find a balance between the male and female. What do we mean by balance? The masculine side will ask you to push something through, to make it happen, to put your nose to the grindstone, be disciplined, charge ahead, and focus. It's important not to move so quickly that you don't see opportunities waving at you from the other side of the road. If you hit a roadblock, use your feminine creativity and intuition to get around it, but keep moving in the direction of your dreams. When Madonna was rejected by a record executive (who eventually represented her), she went to his hospital room with hundreds of reasons why he should sign her and convinced him of her pop star hunger. When Cindy Crawford took a stab at acting with less-than-fantastic results, she took a personal note about her talents, had a laugh, and broadened her reach into other ventures. Now she has her own skin care line and hasn't touched a script since. The feminine allows you to be flexible and open to changes in direction, to overcome obstacles, and to be very resourceful in the face of adversity or rejection. The feminine encourages you to never give up, and when you take this approach, success is bound to find you.

Making Your Hit List

Ask yourself what you can do now to take your project to the next level. Note, it doesn't have to be *all* the things that would take it to the next level, just whatever you think of at that moment. You can always add to it. If it's researching a Web designer you can afford, then write that down. If it's finding an illustrator to draw a character on your business cards, put that down. If it's meeting an agent who will represent you, make a note. Write these down and keep the list in your purse, on your fridge, or by your bedside. Be disciplined about making your game plan but don't be as concerned about the order. Many of us say we want to sell a script, change jobs, get married, or lose weight, but we don't create an action plan to do it. This list is your guide and will change over time; the feminine allows you to be more flexible. Celebrate as things get checked off, as they evolve, or even as they change so drastically that they no longer belong on your list! Some people make lists, start to act on them, and then realize, "Hey, this isn't really what I want to do." One woman who wanted to be a writer realized that blank pages are just too hard to change, and someone who wanted to open a wine shop decided there were too many hoops to jump through and went online. Changing direction isn't failure, it's just a recognition of what you don't want, which always brings you closer to what you do want.

Your list is your springboard to action, but you don't have to do all the work alone. Take a look at your list and ask, "What can I outsource? What can I delegate? Who do I know who could help me meet this person?" Be creative and industrious with your list. If you want to design jewelry, start with a beading class. If you want to work in real estate, talk to those who do. If you want to make cashmere sweaters, see who the competition is and what they say about it. There is always something you can do to get closer to your goal.

Say Yes

One way to take positive action is to say yes. Hear ideas you would normally discount, go to dinner once in a while with a group you might not know, or make (and keep) a date just because you never know what will happen. It's a lot easier to say no, but no shuts you out of a learning experience, an opportunity to broaden your horizons, and possibly a good time. Saying yes is an aspect of feminine flexibility because you may change the direction or pace of your launching. Saying yes will present opportunities. Business school compels students to focus on analysis and plans, and women in particular sometimes stop taking action because they think they have to have the right plan before they move forward. If they do put together the right plan, then they feel they have to follow it lockstep. Saying yes allows you to be flexible and change plans as needed. In fact, there are things that can happen during the launching process that you could not have foreseen.

Saying Yes for a Change

The owner of a newly launched brand of baby clothes is toiling away in her San Francisco town house. With two little kids and a husband, she has her hands full starting a company, especially because she has no background in retail. A friend invites her to Los Angeles for a girls' spa getaway weekend. Looking around at her messy kitchen and three weeks' worth of unopened mail, and remembering a PTA meeting, and an appointment with the cable guy, she grimaces. How could she leave with so much to deal with? But being a yes, as she'd been told to be in her Incubator, was on her mind. She booked the ticket. Her husband took the kids, the cable guy was rescheduled, the dishes stayed dirty, and the mail remained unopened, but guess what? While in Los Angeles, she met a rep for infant and baby gear, saw a handful of stores who could potentially carry her brand, reconnected with a high school friend who agreed to design her Web site, and spent four solid hours fully relaxed, something she'd not experienced since her first baby was born! She arrived home feeling stronger, invigorated about her fledgling business and, ready to take on the kids, the kitchen, and the bills, and all without neck tension or the feeling of impending doom. Her radiance and rejuvenated demeanor were indescribably attractive. Sometimes movement is small. Sometimes it's big. Yes puts out a different signal, propels you, and is likely to attract different opportunities. You usually can't imagine what until you start saying it!

. . .

Portrait of a Lady

Brooke Emery, founder of Attraction Boutique, is a newly minted attraction strategist working with people to attract their desires through workshops and one-on-one sessions that focus on creating strategic attraction plans, meditation, collaging, and more. She had ten years of experience in many different workshops, including being a Reiki master, as well as an extensive background in business marketing. When we asked her to speak at one of our ongoing Incubator meetings about her theories on attraction, even though she had barely begun the process of formally putting her new workshops together, she said yes without having a plan, a name for her company, or her own workshops scheduled. Within three weeks of the Incubator Ongoing meeting, she scheduled her workshops, designed a logo, built a Web site, and had business cards made, all while uncertain about what to call her new business. She put forth her naming dilemma at the Incubator meeting and received great feedback from Ladies Who Launch members. She had originally thought of calling her business The Art of Attraction, but the women in the Incubator suggested she call it something much more playful and upbeat. After some brainstorming, she came up with Attraction Boutique. As soon as she had a name that she loved, she bought the Web site domain name, tweaked her logo, and was on her way. Her business is thriving with a steady flow of workshops and clients all because she said yes to an opportunity that came her way!

Not Necessarily Linear

Being truly creative is not a linear process, but more a process outward and then upward, which is a woman's strength. In her brilliant book, *The Creative Habit*, the dancer and choreographer Twyla Tharp talks about an exercise she does called Egg, which she engages in to inspire creativity and expand her thinking. It's a great example of how something can actually change shape and progress, without literally moving at all. She curls up into a ball to become as small as possible, or, to look like an egg. Her only way forward is by expanding outward. She finds different ways to move, discovering Tall Egg one day (by straightening her back), or Walking Egg (twisting sideways) the next. For as many years as she's done it, she continues to find new Eggs, and to also use it as a source of unearthing hidden ideas. When tucked into a tiny ball, it's impossible to move very far, yet with nowhere to go, great life-changing ideas come. This is movement, right? But she isn't going anywhere . . . yet she's changing, thinking, moving, reincarnating. The lesson is that forward movement doesn't always look like the linear movement we're used to seeing in the world. It doesn't always mean the deal gets done or the sale closed. Forward movement, as we define it, is thought that translates into some type of action that literally can take place in any area of your life, sometimes in unexpected ways and producing unanticipated ripple effects.

You must be flexible as you move toward your goals. You may have the best intentions for a plan, and be set to execute it in a certain way, but then something arises that requires a different or unexpected action. Being able to shift gears or direction to take advantage of a new opportunity is allowing intuitive action to guide you.

Imagine that taking action is like venturing into uncharted territory; there is no path to follow because you have to find the way yourself. You are an explorer and, like all adventurous souls, you have to determine which is the best road and what to do when you get into a thick forest or you encounter a fork in the trail. The great news is that you have your compass (your intuition), and there is always more than one option. You might go in one direction and discover a cliff and have to figure out an alternate route. You may come to a river and have to find your way across. Just like an explorer forging new tracks, launching feels scary, exhilarating, challenging, and deliriously joyful.

Getting Unstuck

Everyone gets stuck for a variety of reasons. They may be paralyzed by fear, moving too fast, not listening to themselves, or lack motivation.

Here's how to get moving again:

1. Make a list of where you want to go, what you want around you, what you'd like to have.
2. Take action on one of these items, even in a small way.
3. Change directions. If you're running into roadblocks, un-returned calls, or unreceptive ears, change your tack. Maybe today is meant for cleaning the house or running errands. Tomorrow may be entirely different.
4. Slow down. This appears counterintuitive because it seems we have to keep moving to get anywhere. But slowing down allows your creativity to breathe. You'll be surprised to see what happens during this downtime. This could mean taking a walk, a nap, going to yoga, or planning a vacation. It's a break in your routine, or something that creates space.
5. Do the thing you dread the most first: make that phone call, craft that e-mail, and schedule that meeting. You will probably discover that it wasn't as daunting as you thought; doing that thing may move you in a new direction, even one you did not expect.

Launchwork

This homework is designed to get you in action and moving forward.

Write your press release. For immediate release: your life! This is one of the most important and profound exercises we are going to ask you to do. Imagine yourself six months, a year, or five years into the future and then craft a release about your project. This is an opportunity to promote yourself and your product—don't hold back! While this isn't an actual release that you will send to the media, it's a great opportunity to practice touting your accomplishment. You can write this press release on any topic, from being the It girl in your city to launching a media empire. Don't follow the conventional models of press releases. In fact, erase them from your memory! You can think much bigger than that. You can even write one that feels more "day in the life." For instance, "I woke up next to my gorgeous husband and leaped to answer my cell phone, Maria Shriver was calling to see if I wanted to speak at the Governors Conference."

The following is an example for you to follow of a mock press release written by a woman in one of our Incubators. While the TV show hasn't happened yet, it sure sounds real to us.

FOR IMMEDIATE RELEASE
HGTV PRESENTS "DESIGNING GIRLFRIENDS"

Atlanta, GA—Do we really want to endure another HGTV reality designer show to make us all feel overwhelmed and incompetent? Yes, actually we do—but with a twist! Tune in this Sunday, October 9, and you will find yourself enthralled and motivated by the designer duo Kelly Kole and Joann Kandrac, who launched Kandrac & Kole Interior Designs just three years ago.

Designing Girlfriends is a show featuring two gal pal designers who, with a take-your-shoes-off and roll-up-your-sleeves approach, transform homes in a fun and stylish way. Always budget-conscious, but never sacrificing their desired vision, Kandrac and Kole enter the homes of ever-weary clients and make them feel instantly comfortable.

"Thank you so so much for all your wonderful help and guidance," said Hilary Smith, a client on the first episode. "The colors you chose are *yummy!* It is amazing to meet people like you two, and right off the bat, I loved being around you. *And* not to mention you seem to know exactly what I like or want. I had the best time working with you." These types of emotions are readily expressed by homeowners wistful for a makeover, but scared off by the reputation of designer divas who will spend your money in the blink of an eye without regard to *your* personal desires or lifestyle.

Another homeowner, Laura Gilmore, said it best: "These

women could really be *my* girlfriends. I had interviewed several designers, but Kelly and Joann were the first ones that actually made me believe that they would stay true to my requests and create a home that was stylish and unique but also comfortable. They work very hard for their clients while laughing and having fun all the while."

This season is sure to be a success for the designing girlfriends, who tackle the requests of clients from ages four to sixty-five, as well as indoor and outdoor spaces. So grab a glass of wine, take off your shoes, and get ready to join in for some inspirational and fun design ideas for your home.

Designing Girlfriends premieres this Sunday, October 9, on HGTV.

Create a road map. Make a master list of all the work you think you need to do on your project at this moment. Do not worry about the order, just get it all out on paper. This list will change and evolve as your project grows, but it helps to get everything down and out of your head. You can then take steps in the direction that feels the best. Pay attention to what intuitively strikes a chord as to what to tackle first. For example, if your project is to become a stage actress on Broadway, then your list could include signing up for acting classes, investigating local theaters, getting headshots, finding an agent, reading the classic plays, seeing what's on Broadway, and so on. If your vision is to launch a line of essential-oil-based bath products, your list will include seeing who else is doing it and where, what would make your products different, what is out there already that works well but could be improved on, and research on the purest essential oils to use. Your list will get more detailed as your vision unfurls.

Take action. In the next week do at least five things to move your project forward. Your list will be a good guide. Don't judge the size of the action, just make sure that you do the five things. As extra credit, take actions for at least five of your friends, either in a formal or informal structure. Connect them with a good florist, introduce them to someone who could help their business, send a new client their way. Adding movement to those around you is good for them, and also beneficial for you.

Waste some time. Choose your favorite way to take time out. It could be reading your favorite tabloid magazine, sitting in the park watching the clouds roll by, or shopping. Give yourself an hour and see how you feel afterward. Keep track in your journal of the things that you like to do to waste time and make sure to include them in your schedule.

11

. . . .

Destination Four: Celebrate It

Celebrating is the last and final destination on our Ladies Who Launch Incubator journey. No matter what you do, or what you get paid, women, in particular, are not taught to celebrate as a way of life. Our production-oriented society only recognizes monumental achievement and frowns upon taking even a moment for a pat on the back. Should you throw a party because you made one sale? People would think you were crazy. But what if it was your first sale? What if it was your biggest sale? What if it was just a normal sale, but you could get away with being excited, having a martini, and whooping it up, just because. If we're lucky, we take time on a Friday to look back at the week, on New Year's to celebrate the year and our friends, or on our birthday to celebrate ourselves. More likely, when we reflect on what we've done, all we can see is what we do not have in our lives. Why is it that once we get one thing, we don't even stop to acknowledge it before thirsting for the next? We look for what we haven't accomplished, what we could have done better, what we will do next time. This isn't wrong, but it doesn't include the idea that by celebrating our achievements, however big or small, we allow room for more to come in. Instead of saying, "Thank you, Self, for creating such an attractive service that these ten people want to use!" we think, "I can't believe only two people have called me about my new consulting work. I must not be very good, or maybe it just wasn't meant to be." In sales, a world dominated by quotas and quarterly reviews, not meeting your numbers will cause a salesperson's self-esteem to plummet. Both men and women are plagued by what they haven't done. In most businesses or industries it is unacceptable to celebrate a quota that was only half met, even after months of hard work. Most people are operating on a traditional standard that doesn't encourage celebrating what has already been done. We must always be striving for the next hurdle or quota. However, people perform better (notice we didn't say *work* harder), when they feel better, are under less relentless pressure, and know that the work they'd already done was appreciated and good.

If what you have achieved isn't being recognized as wonderful, you won't be open for more to come your way. We beat ourselves up for all that we could have done when that actually isn't productive. Rather than beating yourself up for what you didn't do, celebrate what you did; instead of "I'm so undisciplined and lazy, I only went to yoga once," have a supportive conversation with yourself, "I was able to get to yoga once this week, and although I wanted to go more often, that was perfect, and there's always next week!" We tend to focus on our big goals and spend years chipping away to get there, without much fanfare about the little stuff along the way. Celebrate the small stuff and the big things will come.

Celebrating Your Way to Success

Celebrating your way to success is the final step of our four-step launching process. If you celebrate and enjoy yourself along the way, if you notice each and every accomplishment, when you look back on your journey, no matter the end result, at the very least you've had fun in your life. If you don't celebrate your accomplishments you may labor long and hard and still be disappointed at the end result. It may seem as if fun and celebration would derail the productivity process and slow things down, but celebrating actually increases creativity as well as production. Acknowledgment encourages the creative processes. A forty-something mother of two in Los Angeles had worked tirelessly at a job in graphic design, for a company she didn't much like, while trying to get an arts and crafts business going on the side. Burned out at work and tired from taking care of two kids, she was in a downward cycle of frustration because she felt so underaccomplished. She tolerated her day job with very low satisfaction, and couldn't see the progress on her arts and crafts business because without much time to put into it the advancement was understandably slow. After coming to the Incubator, her day job remained the same, but her attitude shifted. Her craft project became more fun because she was acknowledging the smallest changes in its status. One day she announced, "I've bought the Web domain name!" and the next it was, "I found someone who will host a craft party for me!" Before she joined the Incubator group she couldn't see the forward movement because to her it was so small it seemed insignificant. By incubating with the group, she was encouraged to look for any movement, and after seeing it, she had to report about it! Having accountability to a supportive group of people can get you thinking about your progress in a new way. Her entire energy changed. Her vitality and motivation returned because she could see her steps materializing toward her goal. Before, she was frustrated and dismal. Now, she had motivation and interest, all due to acknowledging the little steps.

There seems to be a myth that says if you celebrate or if you acknowledge the good in your life, somehow you'll jinx yourself. The reality is the opposite. When you acknowledge what you've done you are actually telling the universe that you are ready for more. So, if you recognize the good, you get more good stuff. If you see the ugly, the problems, the lack of money, the hard work, the stress, you get more of that, too. If you always seem to notice how slowly people drive or how loud your street is, that will become bigger. If you're convinced that vendors are always trying to "screw" you, then guess what? They will be. These are self-fulfilling prophecies to notice and redirect.

. . .

Portrait of a Lady

After years of being a television producer, Irene Dooley decided to make a dramatic career shift. She wanted to pursue a career as a magazine writer. She gathered every book on writing and began practicing writing articles about real world stories on her computer. Although she had twenty years of experience in film, she took a job at Cleveland Magazine as an unpaid intern and followed younger women around just to experience the magazine world and see what it was about. Finally, she convinced the editor in chief to assign her her first story and she wrote a truthful and poignant story about a seemingly good family man thrown into a set of debilitating circumstances. Her story was so compelling and good that, unexpectedly, the editors made it a feature. Although an opportunity like this was slow in coming, Irene celebrated and celebrated. The daughter of Polish immigrants, she was used to a European outlook where celebration is part of everyday life. She went to a celebration dinner with her husband where they opened a bottle of wine that he had given her for her fortieth birthday several years earlier. At that time she had made a pact with herself that she would open the wine upon getting published for the first time. Shortly thereafter a new luxury magazine launched in Cleveland and she is now one of their primary writers.

If you think you don't have anything to celebrate you need to take a close look at what you've been doing and achieving. Everyone, even in the worst circumstances, has something to celebrate. If you are not seeing anything it means that your mind is like a cloudy day covering up the beautiful scenery. You have the power to change the weather.

It's easy to celebrate the big victories; your appearance on "The Today Show," your first feature in the Style section of the New York Times, or a huge charity fund-raiser where you raise thousands of dollars. There is nothing too small to celebrate. Sometimes the smallest occurrences are the biggest to note. Shop owners have it right when they frame the first dollar they make at the store. If you want to be on "Oprah," you can celebrate that you met the local newscaster in your city. If you want to get pregnant, you can celebrate that you sat next to three pregnant ladies on the bus, so the good energy must be coming your way. If you want to start your own accounting firm, throw yourself a party after doing your first tax return, and even use it as a way to say "I've launched." Any movement is a sign of things to come and through tiny steps, big things will happen. Shift your focus from being productive to taking pleasure in what has already been created. It doesn't matter if the creation is imperfect, unfinished, or still in process. It was nothing and now it's something, so celebrate.

If you've ever watched the show "Blow Out" with Jonathan Antin, you know Tina Hedges and Beth Ann Catalano, cofounders of Twist New.Brand.Ventures, are the rainmakers behind his product line. They are two amazing Ladies Who Launch. One of the most charming parts of the show is that they celebrate and get truly excited about every little accomplishment along the way. Jonathan and Beth Ann are very emotional, so they cried when they saw the product packaging, when they found out they got their product in Sephora, when they visited the plant where they produce the products, when he first went on QVC, and when they had the launch in Times Square. This is what makes the show compelling, dramatic, and fun to watch. They could have looked at the product and said, "Well, we're no Vidal Sassoon yet," but they looked at every movement with as much joy as if they had reached the pinnacle of success. People who become jaded and overly used to good things happening to them also become uninteresting. People who don't appreciate what they have or get excited about the things they are doing are quite simply just not a lot of fun to be around. They are boring, uninteresting, disengaged, and an energy drain. The truth is, the more you have, and the more you celebrate it, the more you *can* have.

The Benefits of Celebrating

What if we told you that you'd be more attractive and actually be a magnet for more people in your life if you celebrated? People are naturally drawn to others who are having fun and enjoying what they're doing. That attraction can help to build businesses, relationships, and to further inspire creativity. Ever noticed that when someone at a party complains about his life, her job, or his apartment, you just want to move on to the next guest? Complaints zap energy. Some people can complain in a funny way, and this is a lot better than just bemoaning life. However, the people who are the most interesting in the room are the ones who are engaged, interested, happy, and enjoying themselves. This is actually a form of celebrating. The results are important, but these are the kind of people who have fun doing the dishes! They enjoy the process as well as the results. Wouldn't it be nice if we could all find the fun in scooping out the litter box or flossing our teeth? Let attraction be your incentive. The more fun you have doing something, the more pleasing you'll become. You don't have to turn into Mary Poppins! It's more the attitude of fun.

Celebrating also means using the concepts of fun and pleasure to attract others and expedite movement. If you want to sell your hand-crafted line of purses, have a party and give all your friends a discount. Make it fun and the right people will come. If your dream is to start a film company, organize a movie party where you pick a film, watch it with friends, and discuss it later over a home-cooked meal. Invite each friend to bring a friend: there just may be a producer in the mix who can help you get to the next level. The point is, instead of complaining about not being able to break into Hollywood, make your own way by celebrating your love of movies in your own home. Don't complain that no one is buying your purses, invite twenty people to each invite a friend to your purse party and see how you do.

We've been taught not to celebrate and toot our own horn because it's considered bad taste, poor form, bragging, or boasting. We wouldn't encourage you to brag or boast either but we urge you to be in awe of what is being created, and your part of the process. When you celebrate in this way it's inspiring and allows others to feel okay about celebrating as well. Bragging turns people off because it lacks humility and doesn't include anyone else in the good news. When you're feeling great about your progress (and acknowledge it), then the people around you have permission to acknowledge their accomplishments as well.

Anything, done regularly, becomes a habit. Believe it or not, celebrating, when done frequently, also becomes a habit. The more you can look for the good in your life, the more good you see and the more your mind becomes programmed to celebrate it. Celebrating doesn't always have to mean "throw a party." Celebrating can mean calling your mom and saying "Yeah! I just made the best brownies of my life!" or treating yourself to a nice dinner simply because you're alive, healthy, and able. Celebrating is any form of positive acknowledgment. A party is the most obvious way to celebrate, but even in writing this book we celebrated along the way by getting massages, traveling to see one another, eating cake with plenty of chocolate frosting, and jumping up and down when our agent, Alison, gave us positive feedback! Much can be fit under the celebration umbrella.

What will it take to get you on the celebration bus? Below are exercises that will show you the way to have more fun in your life, find new ways to celebrate, and make viewing the world through rose-colored glasses an everyday occurrence.

Launchwork

We've outlined the following exercises because if you don't celebrate *you,* who will? Start the party, guests will follow.

An attitude of gratitude. Make a list of one hundred things that you have to celebrate right now! If it seems like too much, you are not celebrating the fact that you had the money to buy this book, or at least a friend to lend it to you, that you paid taxes (because you made money), that you know how to read, that you had a warm meal today, that you made a sale, that you received a phone call from an old friend. Even your bills are cause for celebration because they are evidence of shelter provided, fun had, meals enjoyed, shopping done. Love your bills! They are receipts from a life well lived.

Writing a celebration list can take some practice for some people, or come quite naturally to others. Here is a list from one twenty-eight-year-old woman who was stuck in a job she didn't love, was newly single, had overcome a few health issues over the past year, and was trying to figure out her next career path. She had to work hard at acknowledging the good in her life because her initial response was to complain about being single, hating her job, and not knowing what was next. Here's what her list eventually looked like:

1. I have a job that brings in great money and allows me financial security while I plot my next move.
2. I have dated many people in the past, and know that I am fun, attractive, and a great catch.
3. I have my health and appreciate my body more than ever.
4. I own a home.
5. My boss will write me a great letter of support, whether I need this for independent financing on a new business, or to switch jobs.
6. I have a circle of great friends who love and support me.
7. My parents have offered to bring me and a friend on a relaxing vacation.
8. I have five good books waiting to be read on my nightstand.
9. A cute guy said hello to me at the deli.
10. I waited tables in college and could always do it again while in transition, if necessary.

Make your list. See if you can do this once a week or once a day. It's almost a guarantee that more good stuff will be able to happen once you start celebrating what you already have! For extra credit, look back at your pleasure list from chapter 6 and give yourself some rewards.

Start a celebration e-mail group. Once a week e-mail your friends ten things you are celebrating and tell them how you are celebrating. You will be amazed at how contagious celebrating can be!

Celebrating Party Games. Throw a dinner party for eight to ten couples, twenty single friends, or better yet, a mixture of both. During cocktails, ask each person to write down on a piece of paper one thing they have to celebrate. Watch how some of your friends will say things like: "This is difficult. I don't remember the last thing I was excited about" or "What do you mean by celebrate? Nothing that big has happened in my life lately." Encourage them to find something. There is always something; you can find it by paying attention. This exercise will force them to think about their lives. Are they moving in the direction they want to be going? You will, of course, be in the process of launching a few fun projects in your life, so your celebration statement should be easy. Then, mix up the papers in a bowl or hat, and during dinner, ask each person to randomly pick one out of the bowl or hat. Go around the table, letting each person read their randomly selected piece of paper out loud. Try to guess whose paper fits which of your friends. There will be surprises!

Part III

....

The Ladies Who Launch
Community and Resources

12
·········

Let's Launch Together

Congratulations! You've completed the chapters, are in the glorious throes of launching, and have plotted a new path. When you have a passion and hunger for something, it isn't drudgery; it's a cool and inspiring thing to wake up to everyday. At the end of our in-person Incubators, people are practically flying. We call it the Incubator buzz—people are inspired, connective, and supporting one another. They can't wait to get their projects off the ground.

We want you to know that you aren't alone as you launch. We are right here with you! Ladies Who Launch was designed with you in mind. We spend most of each day thinking about how we can be part of making your dreams come true and how to provide you with the tools, resources, and opportunities you need to launch. Ladies Who Launch is online social networking (think MySpace) meets offline support system (think Weight Watchers for launchers' creativity). We act as a marketing, PR, and distribution channel, but there is so much more that we are planning to do. For example, we could get into finance; we hope to launch a magazine, TV show, and product line as well as a retail component for our Ladies to sell online and possibly in Ladies Who Launch stores. We don't put limits on our imagination, which is why we encourage you to do the same. We will continue to evolve with your needs in mind. In other words, we are walking the talk and living the dream, launching right along with you.

The best, most successful launchers, however, have incredible support systems. Joining a Ladies Who Launch Incubator near you or creating a network of your own will crank your dream or project up to the maximum. If we could tell you every successful launching story we know, you'd be truly (and humbly) overwhelmed. Women can move on an idea in ways that inspire others to do the same. We are all in this together! Each of us has a dream or goal; whether it's achievable within a day or over time, we all want to support one another in making that dream a reality. We could do it alone, but why go solo when you can draw on collective wisdom? We are meant to huddle, talk, envision, encourage, and broaden one another's horizons. You don't have to do this in a formal setting. What if every time you saw a friend you decided *not* to complain about something in your life, and instead chose to conspire with her about your next vacation, the brilliant idea you had in the shower this morning, a cool thought you had about her business, or a stellar idea of your own? There are thousands of ideas to be had, so why not own one?

The Ladies Who Launch way *never ends.* There will be times in your life where you will feel as fulfilled, happy, and excited as you've ever felt. You may feel that you have accomplished everything that you set out to do, but when you've surmounted one hurdle, you will want to always continue expanding your vision and moving forward. Alycea Ungaro is one of the top Pilates gurus in the business, with three books under her belt and her wildly successful Real Pilates studios in Manhattan, and she is looking at expanding her business through products, DVDs, and even podcasting. Your definitions of what fulfilling and interesting means to you will shift and grow as you age, change, marry, have kids, take opportunities, retire, move, and face all that life presents. Hopefully there will never be a point at which you say, "This is it. I'm totally fulfilled and don't want to do anything further to create even more richness in my life." This is like throwing in the creative towel. It's rare to meet a woman who says, "I'm so happy that I couldn't stand to be any happier." We want to enjoy the place we're in, but leave the door open for more great stuff to come along. If you thought your best days were behind you it would be a pretty depressing way to live.

One reason we don't use the word *satisfied* and prefer *fulfilled* in talking about a life worth living is that satisfaction seems to underestimate what's possible. To be satisfied after a meal means you are no longer hungry. Being satisfied with your job means you are generally happy with what you are paid, what you do, who you work with, and so on, and don't entirely need anything more or better. Being fulfilled leaves you room to grow. Satisfaction puts an end to something, rather than lights a fire that can keep burning your whole life long. You were born to dream and to make those dreams come true; the Ladies Who Launch are doing this every day, and so can you.

Your life, your dreams, your aspirations belong to you. Today is a good day to start whatever it is you're burning to do. Today is a good day to take a different route to work. Today is a good day to decide to ignore the voices in your head that say you aren't creative, don't know what your project would be, or maintain that you're too busy to launch anything. You can do more than one thing at a time. You can channel your inner filmmaker by writing a short and filming it one Saturday afternoon. You can release your inner Renoir by taking a painting class, sitting down with watercolors, or buying a sketch pad. What's holding you back? Life is happening so be in it in the fullest way possible, and embrace what you were born to do. There is no one just like you on earth. Even the way you bake cookies is different from the woman next door. The way you wear your hair, the way you talk to your neighbor, the way you give gifts is unique. Make use of all your special, innate qualities; by engaging in the process of launching, every day of the week, you are truly living the biggest life you can. If you were to look back on your life and say what you hoped you did, wouldn't it be great to say I lived to my total, complete, fullest potential. I learned French! I went to Africa! I wrote a book! I ran a marathon! I sent handwritten letters instead of e-mail! I started a business! I went back to school! I looked stylish (almost) every day! I made a million dollars! I was on "Good Morning America"! I raised two smart, beautiful children! There are just millions of ways to express yourself, which is really what launching is all about.

Now you have the tools. You need to be doing great things for yourself and for your life. You know how to get unstuck. You know how to get feedback. You know how to talk about your ideas. You know why women launch differently than men. You know how to recognize self-doubt and you know what to do about it. You know that you're a natural connector. You know that sometimes you need to stop and rest. You know that other people can sometimes imagine bigger things for you than you can imagine for yourself. You know that talking about your ideas makes them bigger. You know that self-esteem is heightened by launching. You know that creating groups around your projects, or Incubators, increases your success rate by huge strides.

What we really hope you know is how real your dreams are and that as soon as right now is the time to launch them. You were born to do something; be someone. Circumstances are different for everyone. Some will come to their project with no financing, no experience, no circle of support, and no self-confidence. Others will come with a few of these, and still others will come in with a helping of everything. Together, as we make our way out into the world with our ideas, realize that you have something to give. You may not even know what that is yet; in fact most don't realize how much they have to give until they find themselves in an Incubator doling out advice, resources, and helpful experience in order to move someone else forward. The more you launch, the more you will fall in love with yourself and your life. You will be irresistible to the very person who needs to love you the most: you. As one husband puts it to his wife every time she leaves the house for a Ladies Who Launch meeting, "To the moon, honey! To the moon!" We'll see you there.

Appendix

Following are some of the resources that we provide on Ladies Who Launch, so join us online or in person and let's continue this launching journey together.

A weekly dose of inspiration. Each week by e-mail, Ladies Who Launch delivers straight to your e-mail box newsletters and in-depth case studies on successful women launchers. These newsletters inspire through stories of women creating their own destiny by following their dreams. By reading these stories of women overcoming obstacles, confronting the hundreds of tiny challenges that they face while chasing a dream, and celebrating when they hit the gold at the end of the rainbow, you can't help but think . . . why not me?

Incubators. In different cities around the country, Incubators give women the chance to activate ideas by using a highly innovative and focused networking method with proven results. Hundreds of women have participated in the Incubator and have launched or expanded their ventures, literally overnight. Incubator members have access to one another through an online network that brings members together nationwide.

Speaker Series. These are quarterly inspirational events offered in select Ladies Who Launch cities nationwide. Come hear speakers who have hit the top and lived to tell the tale. From building brands to negotiating deals, these graceful moguls will get you thinking . . . and inspire you to start doing.

LIVE Events. Yes, the online resources are great, but we know women and we know they like to get out sometimes. Ladies Who Launch LIVE is a day to connect with others to grow your dreams, businesses, and creative projects and to celebrate big ideas, entrepreneurial spirits, and creative talents. Learn from our experts about launching a business, starting from scratch, start-up nuts and bolts, pitching the press, balancing a busy life, creating rewarding relationships, and unconventional approaches to old ways or habits. LIVE events are held in select cities around the world.

Business school. Get your M.I.L.: Masters in Launching degree . . . and your million will follow! Whether that means a million dollars, a million subscribers, a million clients, a million ideas, a million smiles, or a million customers, your Masters in Launching will take you places no M.B.A. program ever could. Take a workshop with one of our Incubator experts—we like to call them MILLie's (Masters in Launching Ladies)—who have earned their expertise by actual real-life experience, and learn everything from pitching the press to finding start-up loopholes, to importing and exporting, to optimizing your Web site, all while balancing your forward movement with your lifestyle. There's nothing our Masters in Launching doesn't cover.

The beauty is that you don't have to apply, you choose a degree that fits your needs, and the best part . . . you don't get graded. All you need is a desire to launch something in your life. The Incubator provides the momentum and vision; the Masters in Launching program provides the tools, resources, and a helping hand.

Advertising and Sponsorships. These allow anyone to target a nationwide market of motivated, entrepreneurial-minded women through dedicated e-mails, ad banners on our weekly e-mails, home page banner rotations, sponsored links, and nationwide events. Women are spending more and more time online as their medium of choice; Ladies Who Launch provides a venue for reaching these women in a personal, reasonably priced, and incredibly compelling way. Reaching this market of women has never been so easy.

Classified listings. For new and growing businesses; Launch Pad, our classified listings section, allows you to promote your products and services on the Ladies Who Launch Web site. Message board announcements that reach the entire network of Ladies Who Launch subscribers and members are sent via e-mail to all of our subscribers once a month. You are able to post discounts, promotions, events, new product launches, services, consultations, and any other benefits you can imagine on this comprehensive bulletin. Can you think of a better way to launch?

Ladies Who Launch Shop. Do you want to sell and showcase your products or services online but without the hassle of creating a Web site? Do you want to drive traffic to your Web site? Now you can take advantage of the hundreds of thousands of women visiting Ladies Who Launch every month who are looking for products and services just like yours. Our Ladies Who Launch Shop allows you to get your products in the right hands and explore the unique and original products from other like-minded launchers. Shopping online has never been so easy or so much fun.

Trunk shows. Shopping online is fun, but sometimes you want to touch, smell, and experience the products in person. Coming to a city near you, the Ladies Who

Launch trunk shows bring you original, beautiful, and useful products created by the women in the Ladies Who Launch Incubator. Check online for cities and stores in your area.

Other Resources

For Financing
Count Me In (www.countmein.org). This nonprofit organization provides loans to women-owned businesses around the country.

For Brand and Name Protection
United States Patent and Trademark Office (www.uspto.gov). You can do preliminary searches on your own to determine if your name has been taken or is being used by someone else.

For Facts and Studies on Women-Owned Businesses
The Center for Women's Business Research (www.womensbusinessresearch.com).

Recommended Reading

For Cleansing
The Raw Food Detox Diet by Natalia Rose

For Motivation
E-Myth Mastery by Michael Gerber
Rich Dad, Poor Dad by Robert Kiyosaki and Sharon L. Lechter
The Secret Door to Success by Florence Scovel Shinn
The Tipping Point by Malcom Gladwell

For Balance
The Modern Girl's Guide to Life or *The Modern Girl's Guide to Motherhood* by Jane Buckingham

For Creative Inspiration
The Creative Habit by Twyla Tharp
Design Your Self by Karim Rashid
2001 Things to Do Before You Die by Dane Sherwood

For Affirmation, Assurance, and Movement Forward
Ask and It Is Given by Esther and Jerry Hicks
Flow: The Psychology of Optimal Experience by Mihaly Csikszentmihalyi
Kaballah and the Power of Dreaming by Catherine Shainberg

For the Truth (Including Scientific Research About Why and How Men and Women Think and Behave Differently)
In a Different Voice by Carol Gilligan
Why Gender Matters by Leonard Sax

Recommended Movies

Baby Boom
The Corporation
How to Marry a Millionaire
In Her Shoes
The Matrix
The Secret
What the Bleep Do We Know?
Working Girl

Index

About the Authors

Victoria Colligan brings a breadth of business expertise and creative experience to Ladies Who Launch. Prior to starting Ladies Who Launch, Victoria worked as director of content and business development for Amsale, a high-end wedding gown designer, where she relaunched their Web site, started an online magazine, and developed numerous strategic partnerships. Before joining Amsale, Victoria was director of business development for the Wedding List, an online and in-store wedding gifts and registry company eventually acquired by Martha Stewart Inc. Victoria began her career as a corporate lawyer at Kelley Drye and Warren in New York. Victoria holds a J.D. and M.B.A. from Case Western Reserve University, and a B.A. with honors from Brown University. Victoria has lived and studied in Madrid and Buenos Aires.

Beth Schoenfeldt is highly trained to work with ladies who are launching. As cofounder of Ladies Who Launch and creator of the flagship Ladies Who Launch Incubator program, Beth has received critical attention from *Vogue, Elle, Essence, Health,* and *New York* magazine as a powerful force in helping people make transitions and design lifestyles that truly reflect their desires and goals. Prior to Ladies Who Launch, Beth launched a highly successful Learning Solutions Company, FLOinc, and developed marketing and sales programs for such companies as Clinique, ibeauty.com, and American Express. Beth is a graduate of Texas A&M with a B.A. in Finance and an M.B.A. from Columbia University.

Amy Swift brings a seasoned and in-depth knowledge of fashion, beauty, and lifestyle products to her work as a copywriter and brand strategist. She is a specialist at connecting with consumers through words and ideas, and is a highly regarded creator of both internal and external brand communications. Brands such as Bath & Body Works, Ralph Lauren, L'Occitane, Virgin Atlantic, MGM/Mirage, Coty, American Express, Tommy Hilfiger, and Christian Dior have all been articulated or positioned by Amy. Her work with personalities such as Dr. Phil, Cindy Crawford, and Christy Turlington, and inside brands such as CNN, Turner Pictures, Sundari, and Puma, has been instrumental in understanding everything from media to well-being. Amy has helped hundreds of small businesses find their voices and is the Ladies Who Launch Incubator leader for Los Angeles. Amy was a contributing editor and stylist at *Contents* magazine, where she profiled personalities such as Robert F. Kennedy Jr., Wyclef Jean, and business leaders such as Diesel's Renzo Rosso. She has also been published in *360*, *New York* magazine, *One World*, and *Cooleh*. Amy is a graduate of the University of the Pacific Bechtel International School.